FRACKING THE UK

ALAN TOOTILL

ISBN: 1482655993
ISBN-13: 978-1482655995

www.alantootill.com

CONTENTS

Introduction

Like many - or most - people in the UK I had little knowledge of shale gas and hydraulic fracturing before 2011, when the first shale gas fracking at Blackpool brought the process to media attention. This was of particular interest to me, because approaching retirement age I had been pondering whether to return to the area of my upbringing, Blackpool and the Fylde.

Because of that link I was particularly interested to find out more about what was going on there. And I found there were plans to turn rural Fylde into an industrial area.

The more I found out, the more I became concerned. Not just regarding my own plans to move back there, but about the area itself. And the more I discovered, the more I realised that shale fracking and related extreme energy production was planned for much more of the UK.

It also became clear that fracking was becoming highly controversial. In the UK it was a new untried technology. And new evidence was emerging about its dangers from the US, Canada and Australia.

This book is an attempt to put together some of what I found through my enquiries into shale gas fracking and related "extreme energy" processes. Most of my research was internet based. Where sources appeared questionable I cross-checked and verified from elsewhere. Much of the original source data - detailed reports on shale gas, including those significant for the UK such as the government's Environment and Climate Change Committee report, the Department for Energy and Climate Change DECC reports on how fracking caused earthquakes at Blackpool, and the report of the Royal Society and Royal Academy of Engineers - is available online in full. So too are many studies and reports from the US and from the European Union. In an age where we see DECC responding to demands for more regulation by bland assurances that they will make oil and gas industry companies publish information on the web, I make no apology for using the internet as an information base.

My opinion, now that it is formed, is that shale gas fracking, Coal Bed Methane (CBM) and Underground Coal Gasification (UCG) are entirely inappropriate for the UK, that they are inherently unsafe, that they would hasten our decline into climate change chaos, and should be unconditionally opposed.

New evidence is emerging almost daily about the environmental damage caused elsewhere by fracking, and new efforts by a rich and powerful industry to exert its will over the common sense of our politicians and the will of the public. I know that by the time this account is published it may already be out-of-date. But I think as a snapshot in time it will stand as a clear warning that shale gas fracking should not be allowed to go ahead.

I have separated the book into the main narrative and appendices for the principal reason that the first part presents the history and argument against fracking as I see it. In the appendices I have added more detail, if anyone needs more convincing, on the influence of the oil and gas industry on decision-makers and scientists.

1 The earthquakes that shouldn't have happened

At around 3.30 am on Friday 1st April 2011 the Blackpool police received a number of calls from frightened residents who reported feeling an earth tremor.

According to the Guardian, one woman heard a loud noise and thought her house had been broken into. Another reported wardrobe doors being flung open. Other people thought it was some April Fool's Day prank. But the police took the reports seriously. They themselves had felt the Bonny Street police station shake.

Police officers were sent to Lytham Road in South Shore, where there were reports of cracks appearing in the road surface of a railway bridge.

At another location, Thornton Gate, temporary traffic lights were knocked down.

The British Geological Survey recorded that the tremor was of magnitude 2.3 ML on the Richter scale, with epicentre between Poulton industrial estate and Carleton.

This wasn't the first time that Blackpool residents had felt earthquakes. Back in 2008, for example, Blackpool was one of several centres feeling the strongest earthquakes in Britain since 1984.

The 2011 'quake was dismissed as "very minor" by BGS head seismologist Brian Baptie, who was quick off the mark in telling the BBC that that the tremor was a relic of a post-glacial uplift from the ice age.

Despite anecdotal evidence to the contrary, he went on to say that no superficial damage would be experienced below a magnitude of 4ML.

But the April 1st 'quake had origins rather more recent than the ice age. Less than two months later, on the 27th May, another 'quake occurred. Although of smaller magnitude than the April 1st event, measured at magnitude 1.5 ML, it was strong enough to be felt in Poulton, and this was sufficient to confirm fears which had been building, that the April 1st event was man-made, not a natural occurrence.

By 1st June Brian Baptie had changed his tune. He told the Guardian that fracking and the two recent Blackpool tremors were quite likely related, because their recorded waveforms were so similar, suggesting they shared a common cause.

The finger was now pointing in one direction, at Cuadrilla Resources, a company which had just started tests of hydraulic fracturing for shale gas at Preese Hall, near the epicentre of the earthquakes.

It was not clear how much, if any, pressure had been applied, or by whom, on the company, but by 1st June Cuadrilla were announcing that they had suspended their operations, and would await information emerging from the BGS data. Mark Miller, the then Chief Executive of Cuadrilla, told the press that *"We take our responsibilities very seriously and that is why we have stopped fracking operations"*.

Later, however, it emerged that in April Cuadrilla had managed to deform the well casing at Preese Hall, which should have put an end to their operation of that well in any event. Cuadrilla finally announced that the well had been abandoned.

The deformation of Cuadrilla's casing was apparently found on the 4th April, three days after the first earthquake. This raises the question of why the well, PH1, was fracked again in May (giving rise to the second earthquake). In the report for DECC published in April 2012 (the Green/Styles/Baptie report) it is stated:

"Once wellbore deformation is observed, a detailed analysis is required in order to use the correct mitigating strategy, which may include either strengthening the casing, or alternatively, allowing more room for greater compliance between the casing and formation."

Can we assume that neither of these occurred before the second fracking and resulting earthquake? Presumably so. But certainly Cuadrilla continued fracking after they had decided that there was no affect on well integrity. It is not clear, then, why they subsequently closed down the same well.

After the earthquakes, Cuadrilla were no doubt hoping that they could resume further drilling and testing operations after a few weeks' lull while the fuss died down. It didn't work out that way.

The BGS data for the second 'quake showed the new epicentre was just one field away, 500m, from the Preese Hall drill site, at a depth of around 2km. On their website they made it official that in their view there was a possible link between the two 'quakes, and the fracking process, particularly in view of the timing. They also made the statement that it was a well-known fact that fluid injection could cause small earthquakes.

This, and Brian Baptie's admission to the Independent that the BGS had installed monitor systems close to the Preese Hall site after 1st April, make it clear that the suspicion was already there after the first 'quake that it was indeed related to fracking.

In the UK the epicentre for natural earthquakes is typically far deeper, at least 10km, according to the Royal Society and Royal Academy of Engineering. The warning signs should have been there. Even the April 1st epicentre was estimated at around only 3.6km depth. These depth figures have a possible margin of error of about 1km.

Perhaps more attention should have been paid to the different depths of the disastrous earthquakes of September 2010 and February 2011 in Christchurch, New Zealand. Although the first 'quake was far more powerful than the second (7.1 against 6.3 - in other words nearly 10 times as powerful and with about 30 times the energy release) it was far less deadly, because the epicentre of the second 'quake was not only closer to Christchurch, but at a much shallower level.

Blackpool people might have reasonably been concerned about the consequences of even small earthquakes at shallow depths and close to the town.

The BGS played down the potential impact of fracking-induced earthquakes, and repeated the suggestion that 'quakes of these small magnitudes were unlikely to be felt. They still hadn't caught on to the fact that the unusually shallow epicentres mean higher perception and damage probability at ground level.

So this was the result of the first attempts at hydraulic fracturing for shale gas in the UK. One earthquake shortly after a fracking started, and another very soon after the resumption of the process.

This was not a good start, neither was it good timing for MP Tim Yeo, Chair of the Parliamentary Committee for Energy and Climate Change ECCC). Four days before the second Blackpool 'quake he had released the Committee's report into shale gas. This was widely taken as endorsing the process. Yeo said:

"There has been a lot of hot air recently about the dangers of shale gas drilling, but our inquiry found no evidence to support the main concern – that UK water supplies would be put at risk."

Yeo's announcement was later criticised by a US Cornell University professor in a letter to the Northern Ireland government as being "myopic and incorrect".

The report did not even consider seismic activity. But it did address concerns which had been raised by organisations including the Tyndall Centre (School of Mechanical, Aerospace and Civil Engineering, University of Manchester, a project with 9 UK university affiliations), WWF-UK, Friends of the Earth and CPRE. These concerns included not only water and air pollution but the potentially far more significant issue of climate change. But Tim Yeo, after dismissing these organisations as producing "hot air", said fracking was safe. Brushing aside climate change implications, his committee's report actually stated that shale gas could reduce carbon dioxide emissions globally, clearly indicating the committee's limited understanding of the issues.

Yeo's conclusion was:

"There appears to be nothing inherently dangerous about the process of 'fracking' itself and as long as the integrity of the well is maintained shale gas extraction should be safe.

The Government's regulatory agencies must of course be vigilant and monitor drilling closely to ensure that air and water quality is not being affected."

The use of the words "appears to be" and "should be" demonstrate the committee's lack of certainty. It illustrates what many of us were thinking at the time, that there was little evidence to support fracking's benefits, mounting evidence of its disbenefits, and that a pro-fracking government was moving forward blindly on the basis of ill-informed optimism. Instead of the precautionary principle, the driving force was political and economic ambition.

But if the earthquakes were bad timing and bad news for Tim Yeo's committee and his incautious endorsement of fracking, they were a gift for fracking's opponents, who suddenly found themselves with a new powerfully emotive argument against shale gas extraction handed to them on a plate. Tim Yeo had in his criticism of opposition to fracking picked out the previous main weapon in the armoury of the anti-shale movement, the film Gasland, by Josh Fox. This 2010 documentary presented problems faced by US areas impacted by fracking. The oft-quoted graphic highlight of the film - water coming out of a kitchen tap being set on fire, demonstrating its contamination by methane - helped make it one of the most forceful environmental films ever.

But of course for Tim Yeo water pollution was not an issue for fracking in the UK: *"Regulations in the UK are stronger than in the States and should stop anything of the sort from happening here."*

The optimism of this statement has been oft-repeated, even after significant reports by respected bodies had shown that UK oil and gas regulation was inadequate for the new onshore unconventional shale gas technology.

In their submissions to the Committee, neither BGS nor the Geological Society of London mentioned any seismic effects. And neither did those agencies which opposed development of shale gas in the UK. This raises the interesting question - why not?

In evidence to the Committee, Professor Richard Selley, of Imperial College London, opened his executive summary with this extraordinary statement:

"There is nothing new in shale gas. It has been produced in the USA for

nearly 200 years."

and continued,

"There is nothing new in artificially fracturing wells. The technology has been used for decades."

So why did a "new" problem only come to light with Cuadrilla's first test drilling?

Whatever the reason for that - and we'll revisit this question later - the Fylde earthquakes turned the tide in the UK. Fracking was now to become a highly contentious issue, and one which would quickly rise up the public and political agenda.

Not only in the Fylde, but all round the country, anti-fracking groups sprang up and started spreading the word, primarily through the social media. If fracking had been below the environmentalists' radar before, that time was over. The pro-frackers, who so far had relied on ignorance and acceptance of their statements, a mixture of deceptive assurances about safety and wildly optimistic views on how shale gas would benefit the UK, found they now were facing a powerful challenge.

The fracking war to inform and win over public opinion had started. The Blackpool earthquakes will be seen as a pivotal moment in UK shale gas exploitation history.

2 New or old as Moses?

Advocates of fracking have attempted to deter politicians and the public from worrying about and investigating fracking by saying that it is an old, well-established practice which has been operating for a long time without any problems. Ergo it is safe. They have also used academics and scientists to promote this deception.

Before going any further it is important to tackle this question, and establish that, in fact, shale gas fracking is significantly different from anything that has been carried out in the UK to date.

Can we trust the academics' views on this?

Professor Richard Selley, with a history of petroleum exploration, related geology, and an interest in shale gas research since at least the 1980s, opened his address to the ECCC, as we have seen, by claiming shale gas had been produced for over 200 years. And that fracking technology has been in use for decades. Fortunately his verbal evidence to the committee modified this somewhat, but his evidence still includes such statements as *"Fracturing, which is a very old technique, as old as Moses, has been used in the oil industry since the 1940s"*.

A template for much of his evidence was *"I am not a plumber; I am a geologist"*. This was typical of the professor's flippant comments to the committee when he was asked questions he wished to avoid. He was not an engineer, he was not an economics expert, he was not an energy expert. He passed on a question about shale gas versus renewables.

In his written evidence he referred, in a page so devoid of content that it hardly deserved an executive summary, mostly to his 1980s work at Imperial College, and to comments (despite his not being an economics expert) on the US oil and gas economy, and ended his brief response to say that UK shale gas may now be commercially pursued, based on the US experience and new techniques available.

Given that the professor's shale gas work is 25 years old, and given that his blurb on Imperial College's Earth Science and Engineering pages ends with *"Now in the springtime of his senility Dick is researching the impact of geology and climate change on viticulture with all the collateral conviviality that such demanding research necessarily entails"*, it does raise the questions of how useful his evidence was, and of how far self-confessed over-the-hill academics with out-of-date knowledge should be allowed to guide politicians.

The question regarding many academics' statements is, of course, how independent is their evidence. Clearly an academic with a lifetime's investment in a subject can be expected to be partial. So too can an academic whose work is funded by the oil and gas industry, which raises other and more serious issues.

To understand why Professor Selley's "executive summary" should be looked on askance, we have to consider a little history. The first shale gas extracted was in 1821 in New York state. The gas reservoir consisted of natural fractures in a shallow rock formation. However this was not extended to commercial and industrial level extraction for another 150 years. Although it is often quoted that the first artificial fracking was in Kansas in 1947, it didn't take off again until interest was revived in the process during the 1970s.

It wasn't before the late 1990s that commercial fracking of the type we are facing in the UK became viable and led to the US shale gas boom. In 2011, therefore, modern fracking had only been in operation for 13-14 years, hardly the age-old or even decades-old timescale the pro-frackers talk about. Serious exploitation of the US main resource Marcellus Shale has only been in progress for some five years since around 2007. The development of the Texas Eagle Ford Shale dates back to 2008.

The reason that this is important is that modern technology fracking is a very different beast from earlier fracking.

Shale gas is referred to generally and by the industry as an "unconventional" resource, as opposed to gas obtained earlier and more easily from "conventional" sources.

The industry will claim that this is a matter only of terminology, but it is important because "unconventional" sources of gas require different techniques.

Shale is a rock formation which is often at a far lower depth beneath the earth's surface than conventional gas-yielding rocks. It is also harder to crack open to allow the gas contained within it to be released. When it is released, from its source rock, gas from shale can migrate naturally to a more porous rock, such as sandstone. Conventional gas sources include sandstone, which is relatively easy to work. But to get at the gas in shale it is necessary to employ a different level of technique.

The first recent development which enabled shale fracking to become viable in the US was horizontal drilling. Drills can now be steered sideways from a vertical well to follow the shale rock formation. The second development is high pressure injection of "slickwater" - a term used for a combination of water, sand and various chemicals. This pressure is required not only because of the depth of the vertical section of the well, but also because of the length of the horizontal, which can extend to between one and two kilometres.

When injected at high pressure, shale opens up and narrow cracks are formed. Sand in the fracking fluid is used to prop open the fissures. Chemicals help to lubricate and facilitate the process. A proportion of the fracking fluid (perhaps only 20%) returns to the surface along with various contaminants collected underground. Following fracturing (which can be repeated when necessary) methane gas can then be collected as it is released.

This is significantly different from earlier fracking because of the extremely high pressures involved, the high volumes of water required, and the cocktail of chemicals in the fracking mix - earlier stimulation or hydraulic fracturing was often carried out with water only.

The majority of the injected fluid does not return to the surface but remains in the ground, which raises the risk of potential contamination of groundwater from later seepage. High pressure shale gas fracking may have unpredictable results in terms of opening up unforeseen existing natural rock fractures. And also, as we now know, high-pressure fracking causes earthquakes. The high water use is also a concern in a world of diminishing clean water sources.

But there's more to the story that means it's not just the technical differences that make shale gas fracking different from conventional gas extraction. Because shale gas is comparatively very difficult to work with, extracting a commercially-viable amount of gas requires more wells. More wells mean more damage to the countryside. Although the surface landscape effect can be alleviated somewhat by the horizontal drilling which allows several wells to be sunk from one central drilling pad, the reality is that to cover an area such as the Bowland Shale basin in the Fylde will need something like 800 to 1200 wells, and even at ten wells per pad this amounts to between 80 and 120 industrial sites in the Fylde countryside. In an area only about 15km square, this is a substantial - and in many people's view unacceptable - industrialisation of a rural area.

Many pro-frackers nevertheless continue to deny that shale fracking is any different from what's gone on before. Can we trust the shale gas industry to tell us the truth?

In the Fylde, Cuadrilla Resources took this to the extreme in order to calm local fears. This inexperienced and new company purchased an existing gas production well which they pass off as their own in the hope that this will give credence to their company, in addition to perpetuating the myth that shale fracking is nothing new.

Cuadrilla presents itself as a British company. But the Cuadrilla network, including Cuadrilla Resources Limited, is owned by Cuadrilla Resource Holdings Ltd, which owns a number of UK and European companies. Cuadrilla Resource Holdings Ltd (CRH) took over a Bermuda company Cuadrilla Resources Corporation Ltd in 2009. The initial investors in CRC were AJ Lucas Group Ltd, an Australian company. When they needed cash to fund the expensive

Cuadrilla operation they got on board the Cayman Islands based Riverstone/Carlyle Global Energy and Power Fund, which paid around 37 million dollars for a 40.9% stake in Cuadrilla. Lucas retained 40.9%, the remaining 18.2% belonging to the management team. In 2010 the 12 directors awarded themselves over 3 million dollars in wages and shares in 2010. In the same period CRH made a loss of over 17 million. By the end of 2012 the company had yet to make a profit. Lucas was getting seriously concerned about Cuadrilla's ability to become profitable, as was described in their EGM report to shareholders in September, and this described their own financial position as precarious, expressing reservations about being able to finance Cuadrilla's future cash calls. They said it was impossible to value their Cuadrilla asset. At that time Cuadrilla was waiting for the government to allow it to resume fracking testing. This moratorium was lifted in late 2012, after which it was reported that Cuadrilla were in talks to secure investment from a new major energy group.

However back in January 2010 Cuadrilla was in optimistic mode. They bought from Warwick Energy their working electricity-production plant at Elswick in the Fylde. This is a conventional gas well of some 4000 feet in depth which has been producing since 1996, and was "stimulated" in 1993. There is an onsite electricity generation facility.

The practical reasons for Cuadrilla making this purchase are unclear. However, it is no doubt significant that this is only a few kilometres from Preese Hall. And certainly Cuadrilla have used Elswick in their promotional activities in the area. In a letter intended to calm Southport's concerns, Cuadrilla wrote to the Southport Visiter (*sic*) that "their" Elswick site had been producing gas since 1993 without any "inconvenience" to the community. This, of course, hides the fact not only that the Elswick site has little to do with shale gas fracking, but implies that Cuadrilla have a track record. In the same letter Miller claimed that BGS had said only one person felt the May 1.5 magnitude 'quake. Actually, only one person was so alarmed by the 'quake that they called the police.

How many others felt the 'quake is quite a different issue, but accuracy hasn't been a hallmark of Cuadrilla's press releases.

Incidentally, in the same letter (August 11th 2011) to the Southport Visiter Cuadrilla Resources CEO Mark Miller also repeated the claim that Cuadrilla's operations were "completely safe".

Cuadrilla's evidence to the ECCC wasn't entirely in accord with this.

"All hydrocarbon exploration, including shale gas exploration, involves potential health, safety and environmental risks. However, these potential risks, which are not unique to shale gas and are common to all hydrocarbon exploration, are mitigated through stringent regulatory requirements and through established operating processes, procedures and controls."

There is a significant difference between risk management and risk elimination. And, as is discussed later, UK regulation is not only far from stringent but not geared up to shale gas operations.

Cuadrilla's use of Elswick - not to mention their ability to distort the truth - is again made crystal clear by Cuadrilla's Health and Safety and Environment director Leon Jennings in a radio interview on 1st February 2013.

Question: *"How do you know it's safe?"*

Jennings: *"There's been millions of fracks performed worldwide, successfully, safely, and environmentally friendly, and a testament to that is the producing well that we have in Elswick that was fractured in 1993 that's been producing gas ever since and there's been no issues with that and that's what we want to advocate."* Eloquently put, Leon.

Regarding Elswick, there was a steady stream of PR intended to draw the casual reader to the conclusion that the proposed shale gas development was the same as had been experienced in the area over the past twenty years. Given that Cuadrilla started talking about many hundreds of wells being necessary in reality, the scale of the proposed development, not merely the distinction between shale gas fracking and conventional gas extraction made their PR seem extremely duplicitous.

In front of the ECCC committee in March 2011 Mark Miller made it appear as though techniques were identical for all gas and oil, hiding the uniqueness of fracking behind some techno-speak.

"The techniques are the same as you would use for a "conventional" well, whether it is an oil or gas well, so the technologies that are out there today that weren't there, say, 20 years ago are related to our ability to locate from surface, using new seismic technologies, the resource, and then to really understand what is going on down hole."

The concerns relating to the technology were, as Miller no doubt knew, not relating to drilling itself but the high-pressure injection of hazardous substances into the earth, unique to shale gas fracking.

But then, Cuadrilla in written evidence to the committee had also said:

"Natural gas produced from shale is commonly referred to as 'unconventional'. It is critical to highlight that the only unconventional aspect of shale gas is the reservoir or rock type in which it is found. Shale gas exploration techniques, including directional drilling and hydraulic fracture stimulation ("fracing"), are conventional and have been used across the oil and gas industry (including previously in the UK) for many decades. What has changed is that these techniques have become progressively more technologically advanced and lower cost over time, allowing exploitation of shale gas at scale to become increasingly economically viable."

This is a clear and damning example of the industry's willingness to mislead. The first shale gas fracking in the UK was done by Cuadrilla later that year at Preese Hall.

The message that shale gas fracking was new seemed finally to have percolated, even to government levels. Whether that was because of public pressure is not clear. The Minister of State, Department of Energy and Climate Change (Mr John Hayes) was forced to concede on 24th October 2012 and said, in an EDM debate:

"It is worth describing a couple of the features of shale gas activity that differentiate it from more conventional oil or gas production: the use of

boreholes that run horizontally through the shale formation, and the creation of permanent fractures in the solid rock along that borehole. Together, these enable the gas to flow more freely into the well, acting in a manner similar to tributaries draining the catchment of a river. The increased concern about these techniques, particularly the creation of fractures—fracking—in north America coincided with the commencement of activities here in the UK in Fylde. Not unreasonably, our communities looked across the Atlantic and were genuinely worried by the reports, although often shown to be exaggerated, of what the impact might be here."

As John Hayes is known to be an avid pro-fracker and a strong opponent of renewable energy, we can only imagine he found it rather uncomfortable to have to deliver this speech.

It also contained the following:

"While shale gas is new to the UK, oil and gas activities are not. Drilling and production has been conducted onshore since the 1930s, and even fracking is an established technology. Few people know that the UK hosts Europe's largest onshore oil field in Dorset, which has been producing oil for over two decades without harm to the environment or the community"

Few people know that Wytch Farm in Dorset is Europe's largest onshore oilfield, for the simple reason that it is not true. Europe's largest onshore oilfield is in Albania.

To describe the Wytch Farm oilfield as "onshore" in any event lacks accuracy. The oilfield itself extends under Poole Harbour and Poole Bay. Only the processing facility is onshore. This makes a difference, seemingly lost on those who either don't know or bend the facts.

Whether the public have been harmed by any incidents at Wytch Farm is unknown, but in 2010 BP suffered an oil leak that caused it to shut down its Wytch Farm operation for quite a time, amid HSE concerns about corrosion in its pipelines.

As an interesting sideline comment, Wytch Farm is unique in that it is the only case where a court has actually been used to apply compulsory purchase orders where a landowner was unwilling to grant access rights under the Mines Working Facilities and Support Act 1966.

A balanced view on this chapter's subject comes from Professor Richard Davies of Durham University, when addressing the Geological Society in 2011.

"You've heard that hydraulic fracturing is a common technique, it's been used from the 1940s. But it is true to say that its widespread deployment with horizontal drilling for shale is a new development, it's being done in large parts of the United States, and therefore because it's being used in a different way, a widespread way, it is appropriate to be cautious and to look at the questions and the areas of concern."

The use of the word "widespread" is significant. In the US, shale gas fracking more than quadrupled between 2007 and 2011. Changes of scale, as well as changes of technology, may bring a whole set of new problems. And a new perspective in looking at cumulative long-term effects. Certainly it has been recognised in the US that the rapidly expanding industry is difficult for regulators to keep up with. In the UK, too, the industry will be greedy for a level of development which we might think is entirely inappropriate for our islands, and for the ability and willingness of our government to react to the challenge.

To me, the conclusions are obvious. Shale gas fracking is a new, significantly different development and extension of mining technology, untested in the UK, and any attempt to convince us otherwise should be viewed with the gravest suspicion. We have to look at it with a completely fresh approach. And if we conclude that as a new technology whose safety is in doubt, its use onshore, especially with the intensive development it would demand, is unthinkable.

I have wondered why US research has been slow in picking up and confirming the dangers inherent in fracking, and why public opposition to fracking in the US has been a quite recent phenomenon. Also I have been challenged as to why, if fracking is so dangerous, there have not been more court cases in the US, a country hardly known for being litigation-shy.

These questions deserve separate attention and I have included discussion of these later in the appendices. For now, I will say that scientific studies of fracking have been hampered by industry influence on government, and the use of undue influence on universities through funding. Despite growing anecdotal evidence of health risks and damage caused by fracking, it has been difficult for individuals to get their voices heard, and their evidence backed by scientific "proof". One reason there have not been as many court cases launched against fracking companies is the lack of adequate law and regulation in the US to define the responsibilities of both the fracking companies and the state or federal regulators. And in many instances potential court cases have been dropped due to out-of-court settlements with conditions of confidentiality being imposed on complainants. But there is sufficient litigation in the pipeline to expose the falsehood that fracking is safe.

3 The big issue

In many ways it is easy for opposition to shale gas fracking to concentrate on the local environmental risks. And there are plenty to choose from. The EU report on risks of fracking (September 2012) assessed all of the following as cumulative ***high risk*** effects:

Groundwater contamination
Surface water contamination
Water resources use
Releases to air
Land take
Risk to biodiversity
Noise impacts
Traffic

The report also assessed visual impact as moderate risk, seismic risks as low.

These risks are real. And whilst it may be true that in some cases, in the future appropriate measures could be taken to reduce some of these risks, they will always be present and it is impossible to eliminate them entirely.

There is, however, one overriding objection that can not be overcome - the issue of climate change.

Supporters of fracking claim that one reason to go down the shale gas route is that its carbon footprint is smaller than that of coal or oil and that this will help in climate change reduction. Therefore, until renewable energy sources can provide energy that is cheap and plentiful, shale gas is the way to go.

Carbon footprint is a handy term, but can be easily mistaken as referring to release only of carbon dioxide. Pro-frackers have often used this argument. However, methane is a more potent greenhouse gas than carbon dioxide. Although shorter lasting in its effect, it is some 72 times more potent a greenhouse gas than CO2 on a 20-year timescale, and 25 times as potent on a century timescale.

A report for the EU published in September 2012 (by UK firm AEA Technology plc) focussed on the climate change implications of shale gas.

The summary said that a number of studies had been carried out on shale gas GHG emissions since 2010, with a wide variety of results. Nevertheless the report concluded that the majority view was that emissions were higher than conventional gas, but lower than coal. The summary describes the deficiencies of the reports examined and goes on to draw the conclusion that electricity generated from shale gas produces GHG gases around 4% to 8% higher than conventional piped gas from within Europe, and that the extra arose primarily in the well completion phase with methane returning to the surface as waste, along with fracking fluid.

This report also confirms that data is simply not available on some of the less quantifiable aspects of methane release. These include unplanned fugitive emissions, and deliberate burning off of waste methane - flaring - during the well drilling and fracking process.

This is not insignificant - the Financial Times has reported that US oil companies are burning off enough gas (as waste product) to power all the homes in Washington and Chicago. In North Dakota, the flared gas rose by about 50% in 2011. Other states show similar surges with Texas issuing 1,963 permits to flare in 2012, against 306 in 2010. The World Bank estimated in October 2012 that gas flaring wastes $50 billion a year.

The flares burning from the shale fields are clearly visible from space. It is cheaper to burn the gas than contribute to the so-called "energy security" of the US. The economics of the process override environmental - and even political - considerations.

US studies on shale gas contribution to climate change are mixed, as the EU report said. There was a sharp divide amongst the professors at Cornell University, when research led by Robert Howarth suggested that fracking wells leaked up to twice as much methane as conventional gas wells. His results, despite the fact his paper had already been peer-reviewed, were disputed in an attack in "Climatic Change" journal, led by his Cornell "colleague" Lawrence M. Cathles III. Howarth returned to the fray to contradict the assertions that his research was flawed and defended his findings.

In January 2013 columnist Andreas Spath of News24 summarised more recent data published in the Journal of Geophysical Research entitled "Hydrocarbon Emissions Characterization in the Colorado Front Range: A pilot study". He reported that the authors found around 4% of all methane production in a Denver field was lost to the air. More data from wider Colorado and Utah suggested the leakage was up to 9%. These excluded any pipeline losses.

If it still remains unproven whether shale gas production is likely to bring positive or negative results for climate change compared with conventional natural gas production, the comparison with coal is clearer, and has been seized on by advocates of shale gas to promote it as a climate-change-friendly solution. It is claimed that shale gas has reduced US greenhouse gas emissions.

In fact the US policy on vehicle efficiency standards will have more effect than shale gas in reducing US GG production.

But the claim is wrong for a different reason. The main effect of shale gas in the US has only been to reduce US coal *burning*. It has had no effect on coal production. The US is simply exporting its surplus coal to the UK, Europe and Asia. US coal is still being burned, but not in the US. Shale gas has therefore on a global basis *increased* production of greenhouse gases, not reduced it.

The surplus US coal pushed down prices on world markets, and caused coal consumption in 2011 to reach its highest level for over 40 years.

The Guardian reported in October 2012 that UK coal consumption had risen by nearly a quarter in a year. Europe, China and India were also burning more coal. Cheap coal from the USA was blamed as the biggest factor in these rises. CNN reported similarly in early February 2013 how disruptive shale gas had become and how it was leading to perverse outcomes across the global energy system.

We can only hope this is a temporary state of affairs. But if in Europe regulation means there may be no future for this coal boom the US will still find markets for its coal elsewhere in the world.

In order to meet the UK targets for greenhouse gas reductions, DECC and the National Grid have developed alternative scenarios for the government to choose from. In DECC's introduction to its 2050 Pathways document published in 2009-2010, the then secretary of state for energy and climate change Chris Huhne said:

"We are committed to reducing greenhouse gas emissions in the UK by at least 80% by 2050, relative to 1990 levels. When we take into account the expected levels of population growth over the period, that means that each person in the UK will need to have a carbon footprint that is about one fifth the size of their current footprint".

He also said *"a successful shift to a low carbon economy requires a clear direction and early action"*. And *"Creating a low carbon economy will require the consent and participation of citizens"*.

Sadly, since then, and with Huhne's departure from the political scene, we have seen no resolve on the part of the UK government to provide such direction. Indeed the recent (December 2012) resumption of shale gas testing sends a single and contrary message, that the government will pursue an energy policy which will not reduce energy demand, but will break greenhouse gas pledges, by prolonging our dependence on fossil fuels.

At the same time as offering tax breaks for investment in fracking, the government was cutting subsidies to the renewable energy sector. In July 2012 the policy energy secretary Ed Davey announced a cut of 10% in subsidies for onshore wind farm development. The Chancellor of the Exchequer George Osborne was said to have argued for a 25% cut. In return for a compromise agreement, Liberal Democrat Davey was said to have had his arm twisted to accept a new generation of gas power stations. In December the plan for up to 30 new gas power stations was announced by the Chancellor.

Widely reported was the outspoken reaction of David Kennedy, chief executive of the Committee on Climate Change, which is charged with charting the lowest cost, lowest risk path to a low carbon economy:

"This would not be economically sensible, and would entail unnecessary costs and price increases. Neither would it be compatible with meeting carbon budgets and the 2050 target. Early decarbonisation of the power sector should be plan A – and the dash for gas Plan Z."

Ed Davey has always been less than enthusiastic about shale gas, at least in theory, but his actions have shown his lack of ability to stick to his principles. In December 2012 he gave the green light for Cuadrilla and others to resume fracking operations. Back in May he had argued that support for shale gas by the Conservatives would undermine energy generation from renewable sources.

This is at the heart of the problem, the big issue. Shale gas will delay the UK development of renewable energy sources such as on- and offshore wind, wave and solar power. Without these there is no hope whatsoever of Britain meeting its 2050 greenhouse gas reduction targets. Worldwide we are heading for climate change disaster.

It has been claimed that with Carbon Capture and Storage we can continue using fossil fuels. But there is little chance now of Britain moving ahead in the short term with developing CCS. In announcing his plan for 30 to 40 new gas power stations, the Chancellor George Osborne made no reference to it. For CCS it was an opportunity lost. The government has pulled the plug on CCS projects, or used delaying tactics, and it is unclear whether funding for these will ever come about. There is no chance without either renewable energy investment or CCS that the UK will meet carbon reduction targets by 2050, far less the 2030 targets. This is not only a UK problem. Worldwide there has not yet been delivered an electricity project with integrated CCS. If we need CCS, no-one is willing to pay for it. It doesn't make anyone rich. I am not advocating CCS. There is a serious environmental risk in pumping carbon dioxide underground at high pressure. It still supports fossil fuel development. But those who say we should continue developing fossil fuels undermine their own argument by not developing CCS. It is now looking unlikely that CCS will ever happen.

Osborne's mind is fixed on the economy, not the environment. But he is wrong about the financial attraction of the dash for gas. Recent research from think tank Cambridge Economics argued that the UK economy would be £20bn a year better off by 2030 if investment were directed towards large-scale offshore wind projects rather than new gas power stations. With an economic benefit as well as an environmental one, adopting a positive wind and other renewables energy strategy would be a win-win situation. It's hard to avoid the conclusion that the refusal to accept this is the result of a powerful oil and gas lobby.

The worst news about onshore shale gas is that it provides no long-term solution to any perceived energy need. There may not be enough down there to last very long. In which case onshore shale is a short term dirty fix. The short answer to the question of how much shale gas there is under UK soil is that at the moment nobody knows. BGS originally quoted an estimate of UK reserves at 5.3 trillion cubic feet.

Shale "resources" means how much gas is underground. This is not the same as available reserves, referring to how much can actually be extracted. Shale doesn't give up its gas easily, and the percentage that can be extracted may be only around 10%. The industry claims higher figures are possible, but this would only be the case with more intensive well drilling.

But assuming BGS was correct, then 5.3 trillion cubic feet would provide about a year's gas supply for the UK.

In 2011 Cuadrilla came up with a new estimate of resource in the Bowland Shale of 200 trillion cubic feet. Assuming a very optimistic recovery rate of 20% this means about 40 trillion cu ft. Or about 11 years' supply of gas. No-one, it seems, knows how they calculated this figure.

More recently DECC and BGS have been promising to release new estimates. After a number of pre-announcements followed by delays, in February 2013 we still don't have the figures, although 300 trillion cu ft has been quoted. So we will have to wait and see what figure the next round of guesswork comes up with. However Cuadrilla's CEO Francis Egan has been trailing the expectation that the new BGS estimates will be in line with Cuadrilla's own. Cynics point to the fact that the BGS is new to such estimating, only producing their first guess in 2008. Also they point to the fact that the government advisor is part-funded by companies involved in the hydraulic fracturing industry, including Chevron, ConocoPhillips, Exxon, BG Group and Schlumberger.

But as yet, there has been no estimate made which suggests that shale gas - which has been in the rocks for some 350 million years - will generate electricity for more than a decade or two, or maybe for forty years if the rate of extraction is reduced. To squander a fuel like this just because it's possible, when it is leading us further along the road to climate change disaster, doesn't make sense. No wonder some of the opponents of fracking use words like ecocidal madness.

Interestingly, the reserves offshore have been said to be many times greater than onshore UK reserves. This raises the question - why then pursue an unpopular desecration of the British countryside if offshore gas is available? Again, it comes down to money. It seems current technology can not produce offshore shale gas at an economic level, i.e. at a level to provide the oil and gas companies with adequately large profits. But if onshore shale is going to be short-lived, we might say if we are keen to exploit shale gas why not wait until offshore technology is better developed?

In fact, Professor Richard Selley told ECCC that he was sure offshore technology is already here, but suspected the only reason for not pursuing this was economic. Nigel Smith, of BGS, offered the Committee a rough guess that the North Sea had five to ten times the shale gas of onshore deposits, but thought we were maybe twenty years off developing the offshore shale. Given that even onshore is not expected to contribute a great deal for the next fifteen years, is potentially environmentally damaging and is meeting increased public opposition, surely the fossil fuel advocates should be giving more attention to offshore. Unless they want a quick profit, regardless of the cost to local communities.

I am not advocating the development of offshore shale gas. But the presence of large offshore reserves just serves to illustrate the weakness of the onshore argument. Offshore or onshore, developing shale gas would be to ignore the climate change imperative. We need a solution to our energy needs - and we could start by taking positive steps to reduce our "needs" - without exploiting more fossil fuels, wherever they are located.

Cornell University's Professor Robert Howarth has no doubts:

"Natural gas burns cleaner than other forms of fuel, the logic goes, releasing less atmosphere-warming CO2. So it's portrayed as a win-win: cheaper, plentiful energy that happens to hurt the planet less than other fossil fuels.

"The fracking cheerleaders are misinformed. Drilling for natural gas has some disastrous environmental consequences. It will speed climate change, not help stave it off."

4 US fracking - seismic events

Whilst I see the climate change argument as overwhelming in making UK fracking completely unacceptable, I acknowledge that it is necessary to build other convincing objections to the practice. As shale gas fracking is untried at commercial development level in the UK, we have to turn to the US experience to examine the possible consequences should the government, in its pursuit of some economic miracle, not be convinced by the climate change argument. And we have to look at the pro-fracking argument.

I think an overwhelming amount of evidence is emerging from the US, and from Canada and Australia, that fracking in the UK would bring significant dangers to environmental and human health.

And there is a growing realisation that in the UK we can not hope to achieve any benefits of fracking that are claimed for our economic and energy security future.

The risks identified in AEA's report for the EU I summarised above at the beginning of chapter three, is daunting. But it is a realistic assessment of the data available to the researchers, which is why we need to turn to the American experience of fracking for evidence. We have no comparison data from Europe. Some of our fellow European states have imposed partial or complete bans or moratoria on fracking. Throughout Europe, significantly, out of some 50 wells fracked, not one of them is in production.

Yet we are told fracking has been going on for decades in the US, and will be safe in the UK. The aspiring fracking companies tell us that this is because there is robust regulation the UK, unlike in the US. Yet their staff came with experience, if any on shale, from US companies who operated to US standards. Their attitudes were formed by US practice.

I want to return to a question about seismic effects - why was the ability of fracking to cause man-made earth tremors not well-documented before the Blackpool incidents? Was there no US evidence? It turns out there was, and plenty.

After the two Blackpool 'quakes it was hard for the UK government to play the issue down, given the suggestion of the link to fracking. Cuadrilla must have known very well by the timing and epicentre location of the earthquake in May, and the damage that was done to their well, that there was a link. They commissioned their own report. It was published in November 2012. It referred to seismic reports from the US (by frackers) and described a rare event of 0.8ML having been detected. They noted higher fracking liquid volumes yielded stronger events. The Cuadrilla report documented two cases of hydro-frac treatment causing events from "massive" fracking treatments in Oklahoma, but commented that the two Blackpool 'quakes were "exceptional". The report says that in addition to the two main events another 48 much weaker events were recorded by BGS.

It would take an expert to evaluate the detailed report, but the summary is clear. Fracking caused the 'quakes, and could reoccur.

DECC also commissioned a report from "independent experts" Dr Christopher A Green, of Gfrac Technologies, Professor Peter Styles of Keele University, and Dr Brian J Baptie of BGS. Their report, which contained recommendations for action, was published in April 2012. It confirmed the conclusions of Cuadrilla's studies, as regards the cause of the Blackpool 'quakes. However they disagreed with the conclusion that the risk of reoccurrence was low. Cuadrilla's report had failed to identify a causative geological fault. And it was entirely possible that there were similar critically stressed faults elsewhere in the basin. They recommended implementing a "traffic light" warning system with trigger substantially less than Cuadrilla's expert had suggested. They suggested an additional batch of recommendations for action, including a lot more seismic monitoring before any fracking was attempted elsewhere.

Detail apart, this was a clear signal, the first definitive attribution of 'quakes to fracking.

Once this was public knowledge, seeing an opportunity, US geologists leapt onto the bandwagon.

Within a year there were a number of new reports published which pointed to fracking causing 'quakes in the US. A few examples:

Huffington Post on July 8th 2012 reported that a new study on the Barnet shale suggested fracking triggered earthquakes more commonly than had been previously thought.

On September 6th 2012 CBC news British Columbia, Canada reported that a spate of small earthquakes in BC were caused by fracking, according to the province's regulator, between 2009 and 2011.

From Texas came reports in October 2012 that three "unusual" earthquakes that had rocked a Dallas suburb may be connected to fracking operations, according to a local geophysicist. The 'quakes were of magnitudes 3.4, 3.1 and 2.1.

It became clear after the Blackpool experience that geophysicists in the US could - and should - have had more confidence in their earlier suspicions. The town of Cleburne, south of Fort Worth, Texas, experienced a wave of small earthquakes in 2009. The industry said there was no link with fracking and geophysicists couldn't prove a link at the time. Cliff Frohlich, a University of Texas geophysicist had co-authored a 2003 book on Texas earthquakes where he found 22 of 130 earthquakes he studied were probably caused by oil and gas production or other human activity.

An interesting report by Reuters (15th June 2012) referred to a new study by the National Research Council pointing to wider industry-related activities potentially causing seismic events. This down-played the ability of fracking itself to trigger seismic events, but described the practice of disposal of fracking waste by pressure injection into waste wells as being more risky. Geothermal energy and CCS operations were also considered to offer seismic risks.

In early January 2012 Reuters reported that Ohio had suspended operations at five deep wells used to dispose of fracking-related fluids after nearly a dozen earthquakes near the town of Youngstown. The measure was taken after a 4.0 'quake.

John Armbruster, a seismologist with Columbia University's Lamont-Doherty Earth Observatory who studied the 'quakes, told news agency AFP the link with the injection wells was "persuasive".

In November 2012 Ohio decided to continue granting permits after approving new rules for injection well construction. Environmentalists were unhappy, not only about earthquake risk, but about the risks of water contamination. Four new permits were issued. Another 31 are pending.

Many of Ohio's 179 waste disposal wells deal with out-of-state waste rather than results of Ohio fracking activity. Ohio is a dumping ground for much of Pennsylvania's waste. Brian Lutz, assistant professor of biogeochemistry at Kent State University, told a Beacon Journal staff writer in January 2013 that the huge volume of water that needed transporting and treatment threatened to overwhelm disposal capacity. He warned of the environmental costs of boosting domestic energy production.

In the state of Ohio 2% of oil field by-product brine is legally spread on roads for dust and ice control. It cannot ban such wastes because they are inter-state commerce protected by the US constitution.

Ohio's temporary ban followed Arkansas action in 2011 to ban current and future injection wells. A class action lawsuit continued. In this case the complaint was damage and property value loss through earthquakes. A researcher from the Arkansas Geological Survey reported a decline in seismic events after the ban was implemented.

In late January 2013 the town of Timpson in Texas started experiencing a sequence of earthquakes, of magnitude 4.1 on 25th January, 2.8 on 27th January, and 2.7 on 1st February. There were reports of minor damage. Timpson is in the middle of a drilling and fracking waste disposal well area. The town had experienced a series of earthquakes up to 4.8 magnitude in May 2012. At that time Gary Patterson of the U.S. Geological Survey in Memphis is reported as saying survey geologists are baffled by the event. He says, "It's not where we normally see earthquakes in Texas."

The cat was out of the bag. Not just in the UK, but in the US. Fracking and its directly-related activities caused seismic events. Why did it take so long for US scientists and researchers to latch on to this? Was it that they knew already but hadn't published their findings? And if that was the case, why were they keeping quiet?

The pro-frackers have always resisted any attempts to publicise criticism of the process. Bad experiences or incident reports were dismissed as anecdotal. They could point to the lack of peer-reviewed scientific evidence to back claims of damage to health, property, water and environment. Indeed they could point to reports which defended their claims that fracking was safe.

The first reason for that was simply that fracking was too new - despite industry claims of a long-established process. The problems arising from fracking were not always immediately visible.

Even avid pro-fracker Nick Grealy who publishes the web site No Hot Air says on his website that if Cuadrilla seemed ahead of the game in bidding for PEDLs in 2008 that isn't surprising, since shale technology was only becoming widely known in the US and big investment by oil majors had yet to happen.

Grealy's interest in shale started the same year. How knowledgeable he is, how much research he has considered and therefore how reliable his statements are, may be judged from the what he said in June 2012 after publication of a report from the Royal Academy and Royal Society of Engineers:

"The Cuadrilla incidents were the only ones in the world where fracking appeared to cause earthquakes".

This ignores the earlier report in November 2011 from the Oklahoma Geological Society which considered 'quakes in the US Eola field, Garvin County, Oklahoma, as being possibly linked to fracking, and described them as having been shallow and "unique" in character. These similarities with the Blackpool 'quakes did not escape the attention of the UK Durham Energy Institute's Professor Richard Davies.

Other reasons for the dangers of fracking being hidden from view include the ignorance of US governments, particularly state governments, the lobbying power of the industry, and the fact that a majority of non-governmental research into fracking and related subjects is funded by the oil and gas industry. It would not be surprising if academics or scientists chose not to bite the hand that fed them.

In the face of governmental complicity - after all fracking is seen as bringing substantial economic benefit in the US - and the strong tactics of the industry and its supporters, it now seems natural with hindsight that it took time for US opposition to grow, and for state and country-wide awareness to present a threat to the industry's activities.

The significance of the UK report on seismicity and the Blackpool events is not that it demonstrates a significant hazard in Britain to people or property, although it may constitute a serious threat to well integrity. It does however demonstrate that the industry has up to now been acting in total disregard of the possible seismic consequences of fracking and the related practice in the US of waste-water injection. It also indicates that a similar state of denial might exist when it comes to other dangers of fracking.

The UK is relatively free from other than minor earthquakes. Not so Italy. In 2012 a series of serious earthquakes and aftershocks in Emilia Romagna claimed life and caused substantial damage. Between 20th May and 12th June there were more than 30 tremors of over 4.0ML. It was later estimated that the economic and physical damage cost could amount to 4 billion euro.

Anti-frackers were quick to ask the question whether the earthquakes were fracking related. Certainly they were of unusual strength for the area and resulted in an upgrade of its risk category. The Po Valley is known for its oilfields, and has been identified as a potential shale gas exploration area. Unfortunately the Italian government is less than open, although it is commonly assumed there is no fracking happening in Italy, but it is difficult to establish the truth. However, on the 1st June the Italian government pulled the plug on work to build a huge underground gas storage facility at Rivara. The 3.2 billion-cubic-meter gas storage project was a joint venture between the UK's Independent Resources and Italian energy group ERG, which holds a 15% stake. The location is at the centre of the earthquake cluster.

Clearly the message is that it is unwise to employ fracking or any other extensive drilling and injection process in an area subject to earthquakes, or near large gas storage facilities.

In the Fylde there is an as yet (February 2013) undecided planning application for a large gas storage facility at Preesall, just a few kilometres from the area where fracking is proposed. Similar applications have previously failed. The Planning Inspectorate were expected to come to a decision in early 2013.

The application (independent of any shale gas application) is for an underground gas storage facility to hold up to 900 million cubic metres of gas, in 19 mined caverns 220m below ground, and for seven multiple wellhead compounds to crate the caverns and later connect the gas manifolds, plus a gas compressor compound comprising pig launchers and receivers, and slug catchers above ground.

We might find the technical terms amusing if we didn't wonder whether any joined-up thinking will be employed to consider the folly of creating a huge underground gas storage facility in proximity to an area planned for fracking.

If the seismic consequences of fracking had been ignored or covered up, and it is only now that considerable data is emerging on seismic effects in the USA and Canada, this demands a critical look at the *other* risks associated with the process. And challenges the credibility of the claims of the fracking companies that experience shows their operations are safe. But viewing the evidence, the conclusion a reasonable person may come to is that so far we have only seen the tip of a potential disaster iceberg.

5 US fracking - groundwater

Put simply, groundwater is water located underground in aquifers, rock formations from which it is possible to tap the stored water with ease. UK groundwater aquifers provide the majority of public water supplies in the South East of England. In other areas groundwater also provides a substantial proportion of water supply. Worldwide, groundwater provides the majority of the earth's fresh water. Groundwater can return to the surface in a natural way, and can be replenished from surface water, gravitating downwards. But these natural movements are slow, and groundwater quality is likewise slow to change naturally. The effects of some human activity, for example, intensive agriculture, where nitrates are released from the surface and percolate downwards, are slow, but build up inevitable problems for the future.

There are two main concerns about groundwater. One is overuse. A human extraction rate greater than natural replenishment is not sustainable. Globally, groundwater use is outpacing supply, particularly in a number of countries including the US. Linked with this problem of supply is concern about the effect on groundwater not only in total but in terms of quality. For example one of the potential threats to groundwater from climate change is that higher sea levels could increase the salinity of groundwater in low-lying UK coastal areas, as sea water could penetrate the aquifers.

Fracking has potential implications for both groundwater quantity and quality. Fracking requires a large amount of fresh water. But most criticism of fracking is the danger it presents of polluting groundwater, and polluting it fast. Once groundwater aquifers become polluted with contaminants the effects will be extremely long lasting, if not permanent.

There is no doubt that fracking uses large quantities of water. As a well may be fracked several times over its lifespan it is difficult to pin down just how much one well would use. It is also possible that some returned fracking waste water could be re-used, although since only a small percentage of injected fracking mixture returns to the surface soon after fracking, again it is difficult to state with accuracy in advance how much fresh water a well would consume. Each fracking may require up to five million gallons of water, or 19,000 cubic metres. Cuadrilla gave the ECCC an estimate of around 12,000 cubic metres. Drilling also requires water, maybe 1,000 cubic metres for the drilling process.

The fact that this could add up to a significant amount prompted the ECCC to express concern that abstraction of such large volumes of water for fracking, and subsequent lowering of the water table, could also affect water quality by causing undesirable chemical contamination and changes encouraging bacterial growth, resulting in taste and odour problems, and could cause upwell of lower quality water or lead to subsidence and geological destabilisation.

Unsurprisingly the pro-frackers told the Committee that these fears were unfounded. Nick Grealy said:

"Three million gallons sounds alarming [...] four million gallons is the irrigation for a golf course for 28 days".

This - presumably accepted without any attempt by the committee to check - is simply not true. The Royal Lytham & St Annes, which as a prestigious golf club, and hosting the British Golf Open, might be expected to maintain its greens to the highest standard, uses 5,000 cubic metres of water for irrigation *per annum*. (Source - RL guide to the environmental management of the links, 2012). This compares with Grealy's 12,000 cubic metres *per frack*. Mr Grealy has a disturbingly sad grasp of mathematics. What he told the Select Committee was wrong by a factor of some 3,000 per cent. There are lies, damned lies, and Nick Grealy statistics.

The pro-frackers argue that despite many thousands of wells having been drilled and fracked in the US there is no scientifically accepted and documented instance of fracking contaminating groundwater. This is a view which is at best contestable. In fact reports from the US flatly contradict this statement. It all depends what you mean by fracking. If you take it in a very narrow sense to mean the actual act of fracturing, that is one thing. That is how the industry use it in their claims. If you take it in the wider sense, in terms of the whole event cycle of fracking well activity from initial drilling to well abandonment and beyond, that is a different thing entirely.

A report was produced in August 2011, "State Oil and Gas Agency – Groundwater Investigations And Their Role in Advancing Regulatory Reforms A Two-State Review: Ohio and Texas", by Scott Kell, Professional Geologist. The report was commissioned by the Ground Water Research and Education Council (GWPREF), which is a not-for-profit corporation dedicated to conducting research and education related to the protection of groundwater. The foundation is comprised of a board made up of volunteers from state regulatory agencies who serve as members of the Groundwater Protection Council Board of Directors. Scott Kell has thirty years of state regulatory experience with the Ohio Department of Natural Resources, Division of Mineral Resources Management (DMRM), including over 25 years conducting or overseeing agency groundwater investigations.

The report details instances of well failure and groundwater contamination. In particular we read: that DMRM identified 12 incidents caused by well construction deficiencies, 11 of those with surface casing corrosion over time, *after* completion of the well.

One incident in 2007 was the result of a deficient primary cement job on the production casing. Compounded by operator error, the fault resulted in gas migration into local aquifers.

All twelve incidents resulted in migration of gas into aquifers and pollution problems with domestic wells.

To pre-empt any pro-fracking argument that it could not happen in the UK, that isn't the issue, I am simply here countering the claim that there is no evidence of groundwater contamination due to gas production activity involving the process of fracking. There is, and this is just one example.

However another significance of this report is that it is the one that Cuadrilla boss Francis Egan used to back up his assertion that *"There is no evidence of aquifer contamination from hydraulic fracturing"*, which was stated in a "community newsletter" in summer 2012.

It is true that the report states that the Texas RRC (Railroad Commission), a Texas Regulatory Agency, didn't identify any incidents of groundwater contamination being due to fracking. And this is what Egan and his fellow frackers rely on. Either Egan can not even read beyond what he wants to hear, or he underestimates the intelligence of his audience. In either case, here he is hoist by his own petard.

Fracking has potential for contaminating groundwater in two or three basic ways. The first is through the release of fracking fluid from horizontal wells, mixed with naturally occurring contaminants released by fracking from the shale, migrating upwards into aquifers through the intervening rock. The second way is the breakdown of wells. Cracked casings or failed cement bonds can release methane or fracking fluid more directly into aquifers. Another significant risk is of surface spills contaminating land, with contaminants sooner or later finding their way downwards into aquifers. When the industry denies contaminating groundwater it is only the first one they have in mind - the direct consequence of fracking. But the other two are the ones raised more often as a concern by experts.

Professor Davies of Durham University has given attention to the first problem. His report published in the journal Marine and Petroleum Geology in April 2012 suggested it was unlikely that fracking at 2 or 3km below the surface would lead to contamination of aquifers lying above the shale gas resources. However he tried to address the question of how far fractures extended from the horizontal wells. This an unanswered question, because whilst a figure for a particular type of shale might be put on the length of fractures caused directly by the fracking, this has to be extended if the artificial fissure reaches a natural pre-existing rock fracture in the layers above the shale.

Professor Davies said if the fracking process was 1 to 2km below aquifers it was unlikely to be a source of groundwater pollution. However he examined evidence that in Wyoming there was a case where fracking had been carried out 600 metres down, and there is now evidence of contamination in the water supply.

Based on this and other observations, Professor Davies recommended that it would be prudent to maintain for new shale exploration areas a minimum distance of vertical separation from aquifers. This should be imposed by regulators, and should be significantly in excess of 600m. He has recommended twice that distance. This was seized on by minister John Hayes. He said on Radio 5 in December 2012 that the Davies report categorically denied that fracking waste could get into the water table. Whether this was through ignorance or through wilful disrespect for the truth is unclear, but is part of a pattern of pro-fracking utterances from John Hayes. The Professor himself refuted Hayes's statement. "We have not proved it could not happen, what we have shown is the safety distance," he said.

Professor Davies led a study which produced a paper in early 2011 on the subject. In the Barnett shale he recorded a maximum upward fracture of 588m, and noted that very few natural or stimulated fractures propagate past 500m. However, the body of the report records that in the Namibe Basin (offshore West Africa) the tallest recorded fracture was reported at 1106m.

His presentation to the Geological Society in June 2012 of his research started off with this engaging comment:

"I hope what you'll get from me is as balanced as possible. I am trying to be as balanced as I possibly can be. I am a scientist and integrity and doing proper science is basically what I am paid to do and that is where I stand on all of these issues."

Personally I find no reason to doubt his sincerity, and I regard him as one of the more trustworthy of our experts.

He continued to describe aquifers as being generally within the first kilometre of the surface, and as a general rule the shale gas reservoirs are a lot deeper.

However, he himself has noted recently and brought to our attention the fact that in Pennsylvania frackers are turning their attention to shallower rock formations. Penneco Oil Co's CEO Ben Wallace is reported by Triblive as saying "What we are doing is unique. It is amazing… It is groundbreaking."

Shallow fracking has indeed been around for some time, at least 20 years, but is becoming more affordable, and legislative loopholes might encourage more of it, particularly from small drillers. Penneco is fracking at a mere 3000 feet down. What price safety of aquifers with this development? A further hazard is that frackers do not have to identify old abandoned wells in the path of their horizontal drillings, and would not be subject to regulations imposing safe horizontal distances from water wells, buildings or waterways on deeper fracking. We may hear more from Richard Davies on this.

Of more immediate relevance to the UK is the possibility of Cuadrilla drilling at Balcombe, Sussex. Cuadrilla have been quiet lately about their plans for West Sussex, no doubt for several reasons, including their preference for easier pickings in Lancashire. Not only does the shale gas field there have greater potential, but Cuadrilla have not met the opposition in Lancashire that they are now facing from the residents of Sussex.

Cuadrilla had put forward plans for fracking at Balcombe. I'll return to the history of this later, but the significant thing for now is that they are, or were, planning to frack at a very shallow distance compared with in Lancashire. Planning documents suggested they were intending to frack at a depth of 2,660 feet depth (810 metres). The local aquifer at Balcombe is reported to be at a depth of 1000 feet (305m) which places the distance between fracking depth and aquifer at far less than the safety distance recommended by Professor Davies.

Professor Davies' interest in the subject was raised when he received a message from an irate scientist thinking that Durham University had authored a report on fracking safety which that scientist disputed. Professor Davies says he did then look at this document - from Duke University, Durham, North Carolina.

This study concluded with a green flag to fracking as regards groundwater contamination. "We found no evidence for contamination of drinking water samples with deep saline brines or fracturing fluids."

Like the scientist who had brought the report to his attention, Professor Davies says he found the report (Osborn et al) to be based on bad science.

The Duke University report received sufficient questions about the validity of its study and findings for the authors to feel it necessary to issue a response which bordered more on apology than rebuttal.

They admitted that pre- and post- sampling was not an option (I have referred elsewhere to the fact that the EPA find it impossible to get industry cooperation on this). But they now admitted that there were significant differences between water near shale gas wells and water further away. The study suggested deep methane (i.e. released by fracking and with a different "fingerprint" from shallow naturally-occurring methane) is migrating into drinking water near shale gas wells. This seems curiously divergent from their previously published conclusion. But then, their earlier conclusion referred to "contaminants" other than methane.

The authors responded to the comment that they did not measure all of the chemicals found in fracking fluids like this: *"True."* The authors admitted they did not test comprehensively for organics or other potential organics in fracking fluids. They now suggested that what was needed was another "joint experiment with industry".

In summary, what was hailed as a study claiming that there was no connection between fracking and groundwater contamination was shown to be flawed, and when re-evaluated by the authors they themselves confirmed the suspicion that the contamination they found, particularly from methane, did indeed originate from the fracking process.

Back in the US a new report on the general issues was published by the National Academy of Sciences, and reported in Business Insider in June 2012.

The report concluded that fracking under the Marcellus Shale may lead to harmful gas or liquids flowing upwards. This seemingly contradicts the industry claim that deeply-buried rock layers will always seal and contain fracking chemicals.

The study found that saline and mineral-rich fluids are seeping into drinking water supplies, although it found no evidence of fracking chemicals doing the same. Robert Jackson, a biology professor at Duke University, said that the biggest implication is the apparent presence of connections from deep underground to the surface.

In April 2012, Tom Myers, a hydrologist, published a paper in the journal 'Groundwater' challenging the common view boasted by the industry, that there are impermeable layers between fracking or deep injection wells. Myers suggested something different, that it is not a matter of whether fluids will move through rock layers but when. And he says the timescale may be far less than previously thought. It may take ten years for problems to become apparent. Even if it takes a hundred years, future generations will face a serious problem.

According to a Daily Mail article in June 2012 by Propublica, an investigative journalism organisation:
"There is no certainty at all in any of this, and whoever tells you the opposite is not telling you the truth," said Stefan Finsterle, a leading hydrogeologist at Lawrence Berkeley National Laboratory who specializes in understanding the properties of rock layers and modelling how fluid flows through them. "You have changed the system with pressure and temperature and fracturing, so you don't know how it will behave."

6 US fracking - how failed wells contaminate groundwater

If there is any dispute about how far and how quickly - or even how - contaminants from fracking activities can migrate upwards through the natural rock barriers between shale rock and aquifers, there is no dispute - or should be none - about the possibility of fractured and damaged wells causing aquifer pollution. So how safe is a well?

In the US standards of well construction and relevant regulation have been variable. Frackers will say that we are safe in the UK. Is this true?

Given the number of wells that would have to be drilled in the UK to satisfy the frackers' demand for gas output, even a one in a thousand chance of well failure would probably mean a disaster for the Fylde. But if in reality the figures were put at one in fifty, that's twenty wells failing. Remembering that an abandoned well is capable of leaking methane forever, not just for the lifetime of the well's production, then if we believe that *all* wells will fail in time we are looking at not just a risky plan for converting Britain's countryside to gas production, but an insane one. In a hundred years one thousand wells leaking methane and other contaminants up to the surface, and through drinking water aquifers, is not an attractive future, to say the least.

The industry claims that with modern standards of technology applying, a triple casing, each casing cemented in place, will render a well safe. However, a triple casing is normally only suggested for the upper portion of a well, with the reduction to a single casing at fracking depth.

Earthquake damage, such as that which deformed Cuadrilla's first fracked well in the Fylde, isn't the only risk.

In November 2012 Cuadrilla admitted that a second well of theirs had failed, at Anna's Road. They had drilled down around 2,000 feet, a third of the way down, when they stopped to cement the top casing. They ran a test on this cement bond, and this apparently showed that the cement had not bonded well between the casing and the rock. Cuadrilla say they punched a hole in the casing and tested the problem by pressurising drilling fluid through. They claim this showed no risk of leakage. However, a packer (a tool used during testing for well integrity) became trapped inside the well. It was not possible to drill further onwards through the lost packer, and Cuadrilla had to abandon the well and cap it.

If, as Cuadrilla claim, the cement bond failure was well below the aquifer, it is not clear why they used an expensive process to check out the well status. A process which, despite being described as vital by some engineers, is still not required by governmental regulation. The Health and Safety Executive has in fact stated that Cement Bond Logging was not necessary. Cuadrilla have carried out no similar check on their other three wells, including the Preese Hall well which was damaged and closed.

So Cuadrilla has two wells failed out of four. Not a good start.

It will be recalled that the EU assessments of risks included an overall verdict of high risk overall rating on groundwater contamination. This was broken down into low risk at well design, casing and cementing, moderate/high during fracturing, high risk during well completion, moderate/high during production, and - less assessable - no classification post abandonment.

One factor they mention is that repeated fracking operations are likely to have a greater effect on well integrity, but there is insufficient data available to assess this.

Something that might be taken up with Cuadrilla as regards long-term integrity of their casings is that the EU risk report mentions a normal ingredient of fracking additives - a corrosion inhibitor. Cuadrilla's short list of additives includes no such item.

The report states that as a difference from conventional hydrocarbon practice, casing material should be compatible with fracturing chemicals (e.g., acids). Casing material must also withstand the higher pressure from fracturing multiple stages.

Further, it states that fracking has the potential to damage cement and may pose a higher risk during multiple refrackings.

Regarding well abandonment, the only suggested requirements are a cement plug at the surface, a plug below the lowest aquifer, and plugs to isolate hydrocarbon injection/disposal intervals.

The report states a requirement for a long-term monitoring programme of abandoned wells. There is no such programme proposed for the UK, and none implemented in the US that I am aware of. In the US even the location of abandoned wells can remain a mystery. In Pennsylvania alone there are more than 180,000 abandoned wells, according to the state Department of Environmental Protection, but it knows the locations of only about 8,000.

Worldwide the industry does not have a good record when it comes to well integrity. One in fifty failures would be extremely optimistic and far away from the scary reality.

Cornell University engineer Anthony Ingraffea, who has been outspoken in blowing the whistle on oil and gas industry practice is rapidly becoming a *bête noir* of the frackers.

He claims that industry studies show that 5 to 7% of all new wells leak. As they age, the figure can rise to between 30 and 50%. Horizontally fracked wells have the worst record.

Offshore oil wells in the Gulf of Mexico report leakage rates of some 60% after 16 years of service. In the North Sea the Norwegian Petroleum Safety Authority reports that 18% of deep offshore oil and gas wells have integrity problems. Australia has chronic leakage problems from fractured coal bed methane (CBM) wells. In Canada, according to industry returns to regulators, about 5% of 300,000 oil and gas wells are leaking. That's 15,000 leaking. But an independent study by Bachu and Watson estimated the percentage for the deviated (i.e. non-vertical) wells rose to perhaps 60%.

Given the risk that high-pressure fracking increases the chance of leaks creating pathways percolating to other wells, the atmosphere and groundwater, these are not encouraging statistics.

Even worse is the conclusion reached by several commentators that *all* wells will fail in time. It's not only Ingraffea who is drawing attention to this. Maybe we should be more worried about decommissioning of North Sea gas because of the pollution and cost implications rather than the effect on the UK's gas supplies.

"There are more leaking wells than people know about, mainly because it is something that companies do not want to advertise," says David Weaver, former managing director of BP Northern Europe Gas, Power and Renewables, and now chief executive of clean-tech company Ultra Green.

"[Underground] there are a lot of gases that speed the ageing process of cement," says Alf Jan Wik, a senior vice-president at WellCem, a Norwegian P&A specialist. *"75% to 80% of wells are leaking worldwide … When you consider that over 10,000 wells have been drilled on the UK continental shelf alone, the cost potential of leaking wells is phenomenal."*

Of course, since there is only a decade or so of wide-scale employment of the new technology of hydraulic fracking, it is not surprising that estimates of long-term well failure vary.

Dr. Ronald Bishop, of State University of New York, College at Oneonta, is a researcher into impacts of shale gas extraction on water quality.

His assessment, following examination of the EPA's reports into leaking oil and gas wells, and survey of drilling practice, is that "the probability that a project scope of as few as ten modern gas wells will impact local ground water within a century approaches 100% certainty."

On this view, it is not a question of whether a well will fail and leak, but when.

It will always be argued that new developments, for example of casing and cement improvements, will help the industry prevent the problems of the past, but looking at the single case of Cuadrilla, and its failure to construct and operate two of its wells successfully, this is not a reassuring argument.

Dr Bishop reports a global rate of blowouts (uncontrolled releases of oil or gas when pressure controls fail) at around 1.5 per thousand wells. National (US) problems with orphan/abandoned wells are about one in six, and the rate of groundwater problems about one in fifty *in the short term.*

Scientists aside, common sense and most reasonable thought will suggest that anything man-made depending on cement and steel will sooner or later fall apart. All wells will fail in time.

A bone of contention between the industry and scientists is over terminology. The industry claim that no groundwater has been contaminated by hydraulic fracturing invites discussion of what is mean by the words "hydraulic fracturing". Do we take this to mean the narrow definition of the comparatively short time of a single fracking operation? This ignores the long-term risks of well failure and leakage, and other activities associated with shale gas extraction, including primary surface problems, problems of transport of chemicals, and handling on the well pad. Compilation of data in the US is complicated by the fact that most incidents are likely in the phase of initial drilling and stimulation. Dr Bishop complains that many existing wells were not documented at this stage.

Dr Bishop does, however, in his 2011 paper "Chemical and Biological Risk Assessment for Natural Gas Extraction in New York" cite ample evidence of fracking contamination incidents.

In Colorado, 1549 spill incidents related to natural gas extraction activities between January 2003 and March 2008, with an estimation (by the Congressional Sportsmen's Foundation) that 20% of those, i.e. 310 incidents, impacted groundwater.

In New Mexico the NM Oil Conservation Division recorded 705 groundwater-contaminating incidents caused by the gas industry between 1990 and 2005.

Data from West Virginia similarly led to a conclusion that there were groundwater impacts from around 1.5% of active gas wells.

The Pennsylvania Land Trust reported 1610 DEP (Department of Environmental Protection) violations in Marcellus shale wells between January 2008 and late August 2010, of which 1052 were judged likely to impact the environment. Dr Bishop works this up to an estimate of 7% shale gas wells having negative environmental impact.

Dr Bishop is far from being a lone voice. There are many further evidences to counter the shale industry's claim that it does not impact groundwater. The US Environmental Protection Agency EPA produced a draft report in late 2011 which provoked an outraged reaction. The report suggested that fracking had contaminated groundwater near Pavillion, Wyoming. This has become a classic case of accusation and denial. Local landowners objected to the smell and taste of their water, and although this wasn't new, the situation got worse when their water turned brown after the start of nearby fracking activity. It wasn't until 2008 that the EPA tested the wells tapping the groundwater above the fracking wells, (some 170 of them). It found evidence of contamination in both shallow and deep wells. The finger was pointed at surface pits storing drilling waste, but this did not explain the contamination of deeper groundwater, where an upward pollution migration was suggested. Problems were found when fracking well cement and casings were examined.

The EPA, after a second round of sampling in 2010, advised residents not to drink the water, and to vent their homes where they bathed because the methane in the water could cause an explosion.

Industry and state officials questioned the findings when the draft report was published. The US Geological Society was asked to conduct a new analysis. This was sent to the state and the EPA in September 2012. The EPA said the new results confirmed its view. Although other scientific opinion was that the results were certainly suggestive of fracking being the source of contamination (by a range of hydrocarbons and chemicals associated with fracking fluids and drilling activities, and high pH levels which suggested solvent use), Encana Corporation, an owner of wells near Pavillion, maintains there is no proof that drilling operations are to blame.

As already mentioned, Senator Jim Inhofe objected loudly to the EPA's study, telling a senate committee that he found the report "offensive". Another example suggesting science is not enough to stop fracking. It's the politicians who lead the rush for gas regardless of consequences. I doubt whether Inhofe was as offended as the residents whose water became unusable.

7 US fracking - surface water and air pollution

The GAO, the US Government Accountability Office, is an independent, non-partisan agency that works for Congress, according to its website. Often called the "congressional watchdog," GAO investigates how the federal government spends taxpayers' dollars.

However, it also addresses other areas of constitutional responsibility. In September 2012 it released a report on oil and gas entitled "Information on Shale Resources, Development, and Environmental and Public Health Risks".

Its findings included acknowledgement that estimates of recoverable shale gas, by the Environmental Information Administration EIA, were now - at 482 trillion cubic feet - an increase of some 280 per cent over the 2008 estimate. It moved on to say:

"Oil and gas development, whether conventional or shale oil and gas, pose inherent environmental and public health risks, but the extent of these risks associated with shale oil and gas development is unknown, in part, because the studies GAO reviewed do not generally take into account the potential long-term, cumulative effects."

With this proviso, the report's summary states that regarding water quality a number of studies and publications GAO reviewed indicate that shale oil and gas development pose risk. The summary list of contamination sources includes erosion from ground disturbance, spills and releases of chemicals and other fluids or underground migration of gas and chemicals.

Regarding air quality, GAO say there are risks including from increased truck traffic, emissions from pumps and other fracking equipment, dust releases, including silica sand particles, flared or vented gas, and unintentional releases of pollutants from faulty equipment or temporary waste impoundments.

A second report from the GAO also released in September 2012, "Unconventional Oil and Gas Development, Key Environmental and Public Health Requirements" looked at federal and state legislation and found that enforcement of existing laws was difficult and limited. The industry was exempted from more general regulation and public health laws, in particular from parts of the Clean Water Act and the Resource Conservation and Recovery (hazardous waste) requirements.

Inspection and enforcement was "challenging" because of, for example, lack of the appropriate background scientific data, and staff problems due to trained staff finding industry jobs better paid.

In a nutshell, the US is finally coming to realise the immense challenges of a fast-developing new industry, and only now appreciating that it is an industry with new environmental and health risks that require urgent action from the regulators and industry alike.

New studies are emerging to back up the general picture and fill out some detail. In August 2012 a report from Stony Brook University, New York found that wastewater from fracking posed substantial risks of river and other water pollution. A university summary of the report says the scientists found "Even in a best case scenario, an individual well would potentially release at least 200 cu. m. of contaminated fluids."

The disposal of used fracking fluids through industrial wastewater treatment facilities could lead to elevated pollution levels in rivers and streams because many such facilities are not designed to handle wastewater containing high concentrations of salts or radioactivity. The report claimed that this problem dwarfed other risks such as tanker spills.

This highlights the fact that when a well is fracked and waste fluid returns to the surface following fracking, it returns with not only a portion of the original fracking chemical cocktail, but with new added ingredients. These can include salts, heavy metals barium and strontium, organic pollutants (for example benzene and toluene) and radium.

These substances are all naturally occurring. But Dr Bishop of the State University of New York has also recorded the appearance in shale gas waste of 4-nitroquinoline-1-oxide, 4-NQO, which he describes as an extremely potent carcinogen. This toxin is not a chemical additive and does not occur naturally in shale. Dr Bishop therefore asks whether chemical interactions caused during the drilling process are responsible for its presence.

Unsurprisingly, radioactivity grabs the most attention. Levels of radioactivity in fracking waste from Marcellus Shale operations have been noted by several agencies. The Marcellus shale has particularly high normally occurring levels of radioactive elements including uranium and thorium, and decay products, particularly radium. The Pennsylvania DEP announced in January 2013 that it will undertake a year-long study into radioactivity occurring in fracking waste and by-products. The DEP was previously complacent about this issue. But more recent reports from the US Geological Survey, and in particular from Penn State University, found waste from fracking can be radioactive. The industry does not appear to dispute this. What is at issue is the amount of radioactivity that may be present in fracking waste, and how it can be disposed of safely. The same issue applies to other waste contaminants.

In the US some practices employed in fracking waste disposal have been showing less than appropriate regard to potential dangers. In some cases this is unlikely to be repeated in the UK. In the US it has not been unusual for returned fracking fluid to be stored in open reservoirs until permanently disposed of. In the UK, in testing to date, returned fracking fluid has been stored in sealed tanks.

Because of the high salinity of returned fracking fluid it has been tempting to dispose of it by spraying as a de-icer (or a dust suppressant) on roads. This has happened - illegally - in the US and in Australia.

But what has been an important - and legal - method of disposal in the US has been injecting waste fracking fluid into waste disposal wells. The hazards of this are now clearer - not only does pumping toxic waste back underground promise problems for the future - it is not credible that eventually the waste will not return to the surface, especially with the high risk of eventual well failure - and it is now recognised that this practice probably has more potential than fracking to cause seismic events.

In the UK we have already seen the difficulties of disposing of even the comparatively small volumes of fracking waste generated by Cuadrilla's Preese Hall operation.

Cuadrilla's evidence to the ECCC during the committee's examination in 2011 referred to earlier was not convincing. At best displaying an ignorance and at worst an arrogant and careless approach, they did not know whether there were adequate waste disposal facilities in the UK for the volumes of waste possibly generated during the exploitation process. And the reference to possible waste disposal well drilling was incredibly casual.

*"**Q (Chair)** If we see shale gas production developing in this country, will there be a need for lots of waste treatment centres as a result of that?*

***Mark Miller:** I don't know; I guess I am not familiar enough yet with how many are out there and where they are at. I have only really looked at what we are using. I suppose it is possible, but the oil and gas industry and a lot of the waste facilities we are using have really been established to handle some of the fluids coming from offshore, and that is a pretty big industry. I don't think the amount that we would be bringing to it, even if shale gas got pretty active, would really exceed the capacity that was set up to service the North Sea.*

***Dennis Carlton:** If indeed it did, we could drill a disposal well or contract with somebody who has a disposal well to increase the volume capacity."*

It is worth digressing to relate that so far what has actually happened to Cuadrilla's waste has not been encouraging.

It was originally understood that Cuadrilla would dispose of waste from Preese Hall to Davyhume in Manchester for treatment. A first batch was delivered, where apparently the Environmental Agency could not decide how to dispose of it, and it remained stored on-site. Later it appeared that the waste was dumped in the Manchester Ship Canal. It is not clear what, if any, treatment it received before disposal.

New regulations introduced in October 2011 regarding radioactive waste meant Cuadrilla could no longer act without more permits. Their later waste still remains on-site at Preese Hall until it is decided how it may be disposed of.

Turning to air pollution, I already touched on the debate regarding release of greenhouse gases. But how else does fracking affect the air?

The US EPA has attempted to address issues of the release of smog and soot forming pollutants, with proposals for new controls on storage tanks, and transmission pipelines. Increases in low level ozone and dangerous levels of cancer-producing benzene are two of the reported problems. Environmental groups were not impressed with the two years the EPA took before putting proposals forward.

Endocrine Disruption Exchange (TEDX) is a non-profit research organization in Colorado which studies the impact of environmental pollutants on the endocrine system, a network of hormone-producing glands that affects nearly every organ in the body. According to Bloomberg, TEDX has spent years studying the health effects of natural gas drilling, and its reports are routinely criticized by the industry.

In December 2012 TEDX reported that over 50 of a set of chemicals called non-methane hydrocarbons, or NMHCs, is found in the air near drilling sites. These affect the brain and nervous system. Some were detected at levels that would potentially harm children exposed to them before birth. The source of the chemicals is likely to be a mix of raw gas that is vented from the wells and emissions from industrial equipment during the gas production process. High concentrations were recorded after drilling of new wells, but these did not significantly increase during production after fracking. There was a message for regulators in the findings - chemical concentrations were below federal exposure limits, but above concentrations found to have health effects in scientific studies.

The TEDX study was inspired by years of complaints from people living near gas wells about headaches and respiratory problems. Many of the symptoms began the moment drilling started, long before the wells were fracked.

It is not only local communities which are at risk from fracking. So too are industry workers. The National Institute for Occupational Safety and Health (NIOSH) records that the oil and gas extraction industry has an annual occupational fatality rate of 27.5 per 100,000 workers (2003-2009) - more than seven times higher than the rate for all US workers. In addition to accident fatalities, traffic accidents were a major factor involved in work-related death. Accident rates are suggested to be partly due to the fact that many workers have limited experience in the industry - a fact that those in the UK who are attracted by the prospect of new shale gas jobs might take into account.

Together with Occupational Safety and Health Administration OSHA, the main federal agency responsible for enforcement of health and safety legislation, NIOSH, issued a hazard alert on "Worker Exposure to Silica during Hydraulic Fracturing".

They had collected 116 samples from fracking pads in five states. Of the 116 samples, 47 showed silica exposures greater than the OSHA calculated permissible exposure limit (PEL), 9% with levels 10 times higher than the PEL. 79% showed exposures greater than NIOSH's recommended exposure limit (REL) and 31% with levels more than 10 times higher than REL. 1 sample was 100 higher than the REL.

Fracking sand contains up to 99% silica. Breathing silica can cause the lung disease silicosis, which can reduce breathing ability. Silica can also cause lung cancer and has been linked to other respiratory and kidney diseases.

Just another example, then, of why neither the UK government nor the regulatory authorities, particularly the HSE, should regard fracking as being no different from any other oil or conventional gas operations.

8 US fracking - water, air and health

"These stories from Pennsylvania are very alarming. The perspective of the gas industry fails to show adequate concern for the long-term health and quality of life of people. When you listen to the personal experiences of actual residents of Pennsylvania and other states where fracking has gone forward, you will hear stories of dead cows, pets, sick children, poisoned water and other serious health and environmental problems."

- Dr. Sheila Bushkin, MD, MPH of the Institute for Health and the Environment at University at Albany. 30/1/2013.

It is tempting to leave this chapter content there. Dr Bushkin says it all. The argument about fracking is not about the scientific validity of studies and reports, it is not about economics, nor about abstract concepts of what constitutes pollution. It is about our society, and our social responsibility. What could be more important than the health of our people, our children and animals, and future generations?

The above quote comes at a time when New York state is ponderously working its way to deciding whether a moratorium on fracking should be lifted. Its neighbour Pennsylvania has borne the brunt of US fracking activities, sharing as it does with NY the huge Marcellus shale resource. Pennsylvania people are coming forward to tell New York - don't do it, don't let what happened to us happen to you. It is unclear just how much effort is being put by New York state to having health risks properly assessed before making a decision on the moratorium, but what seems certain is that they are not allowing sufficient time for a thorough study.

An article from Ecowatch is worth quoting to give an idea of the nature of the reported problems.

"My story is not unusual," said Terry Greenwood, a farmer from Southwestern Pennsylvania. "After my cows drank from a pond that was contaminated by frackwater, 10 of the 19 calves were born stillborn."

"The industry says there are no problems," said Matt Manning. "Well when the industry came to Northeastern PA, our water turned black and started bubbling. Our kids would cough and choke in the shower. It got so bad that the state required the companies to provide us with deliveries of clean water. But that's not a long-term solution."

Ron Gulla, a farmer from Hickory in Southwest Pennsylvania has compiled a growing list of more than 800 individuals who have been harmed by fracking. Gulla said, "These are not isolated incidents. I've talked to so many people whose water has been contaminated and whose families have been poisoned by fracking."

Sue Kinchy, a nurse and more than 30 year resident of Bradford County, PA who fled to New York a year ago after the impacts of fracking had destroyed the nature of her community said, "Medically, we saw fracking linked to rashes, dizziness, headaches, and many, many more accidents. Crime skyrocketed, trucks crowded the roads, and kids went to school within sight of well pads and flaring. Governor Cuomo, don't allow fracking in New York."

David Brown, ScD of the Southwest Pennsylvania Environmental Health Project said in a statement, "With tens of thousands of wells, transportation and processing devices spread across the landscape of the typical gas fields or plays, hundreds of accidents will happen over a year. No one can assure people who live, work, or attend school near drilling and fracking operations that they are safe."

If the stories of health problems and fracking-related incidents and accidents were confined to one small area we might understand if the advocates of fracking deny a single cause and a wider implication for the industry.

But problems are reported from all areas where fracking has taken place. In Texas the huge Barnett Shale resource is being exploited by the shale gas industry. You might expect a state steeped in an oil-producing tradition to have welcomed shale gas as just another step, and adopted it as part of their culture. Indeed some commentators have suggested that the reason that the US anti-fracking movement has burst into life is the involvement of the Eastern states, with their different attitudes and culture.

Yet even in Texas the picture is emerging of a growing dissatisfaction with fracking, and health concerns.

The small town of Dish, 35 miles north of Fort Worth, is one example. The town was previously named Clark, but in 2005 it agreed to change its name in return for a decade of free satellite TV. That wasn't the only change. Energy companies arrived and started fracking.

The population of 200 or so is now complaining of the destruction to their community which fracking has brought about. And they are complaining about health problems ranging from nosebleeds to cancer.

The town spent its own money on an air quality survey. It found elevated levels of several chemicals including benzene. Since then the companies have made changes that according to a state-installed monitoring station has now shown pollution to be within acceptable levels. By then for some it was too late.

Ex-mayor Calvin Tillman became alarmed when his two sons started getting nosebleeds, which seemed to occur when the odours of gas were strongest and monitoring showed high levels of chemicals. Tillman moved his family out of the town. He denies it is an isolated story, and claims that when he polled the town he found about half of the population had a symptom that he could relate to what he knew about the chemicals found.

Tillman appeared in Josh Fox's film Gasland, and now makes tours warning about the dangers of letting frackers move into communities. Whilst it may be argued that Dish's problems were due to poor state regulation and inadequate response from regulators to concerns, it is hard to deny that potential problems of air quality and subsequent health issues may exist.

In the case of Dish, a state study of blood samples taken from residents was inconclusive, and found the levels of numerous chemicals were no different than expected in 95% of the American population. However the investigators themselves admitted that their study was severely limited as a one-time sample.

According to Environmental Health Perspectives (EHP), a monthly journal of peer-reviewed research, about 14,000 wells have been drilled around Fort Worth since the late 1990s. Wilma Subra, president of Subra Company, an environmental group in New Iberia, Louisiana, reports that condensate tanks, used to rid gas of non-methane hydrocarbons, emit compounds such as carbon disulfide which can cause cardiovascular, neurological and hepatic effects with chronic high exposure. When compressors, which help push produced gas through pipelines, undergo maintenance they are evacuated and the contents released or flared directly to the air.

Some residents living near these facilities complain of headaches, diarrhoea, nosebleeds, dizziness, blackouts, muscle spasms, and other problems. But detailed studies into these adverse health effects are lacking, and research conducted to date has yielded conflicting results.

Bernard Goldstein, a professor in the Graduate School of Public Health at the University of Pittsburgh, says they have received many complaints from individuals near fracking operations, but published epidemiologic studies relating shale gas production to health are virtually nonexistent. That makes it difficult to identify causes and effects, and establish whether disease clusters are industry-related as activists might imply. He suggests shale gas development should be accompanied by prospective health research including baseline disease surveillance and environmental monitoring.

If in the UK the Fylde is to suffer the operation of maybe a thousand wells in a small area, this is something the Fylde residents should take up now. After shale gas extraction starts it will be too late.

In Denver, the Colorado School of Public Health has provided perhaps the only serious study as yet of fracking-related air quality and health issues, as a result of rapid fracking expansion in Garfield County.

Researchers found that air pollution caused by hydraulic fracturing may contribute to acute and chronic health problems for those living near natural gas drilling sites.

They emphasised the point that most concern had been expressed about water pollution. In the light of their report, based on three years of monitoring, air pollution needs more attention.

In brief, researchers found a number of potentially toxic petroleum hydrocarbons in the air near the wells, including benzene, ethylbenzene, toluene and xylene. Benzene has been identified as a known carcinogen. Other chemicals included heptane, octane and diethylbenzene but information on their toxicity is limited.

"Our results show that the non-cancer health impacts from air emissions due to natural gas development is greater for residents living closer to wells," the report said. *"The greatest health impact corresponds to the relatively short-term, but high emission, well completion period."*

"We also calculated higher cancer risks for residents living nearer to the wells as compared to those residing further [away]. Benzene is the major contributor to lifetime excess cancer risk from both scenarios."

Lisa McKenzie, Ph.D., MPH, lead author of the study, noted that EPA standards are designed to be public health proactive and may overestimate risks.

"However, there wasn't data available on all the chemicals emitted during the well development process," she said. "If there had been, then it is entirely possible the risks would have been underestimated."

Despite the warning signs, in the US the shale gas industry has not only built wells near communities, but on university campuses and even close to primary and secondary schools.

In 2011 the governor of Pennsylvania, Tom Corbett, suggested offsetting college tuition fees by leasing parts of state-owned college campuses to gas drillers. A year later, he got this signed into law, opening up 14 universities to having their campuses fracked. 50% of the income would stay within the individual university, 35%

would be distributed across the state system, and 15% would subsidise student tuition.

This wouldn't be a first. Campus drilling laws enable colleges in Ohio to allow fracking , and two West Virginia colleges have leased land to frackers. There are also frackers on campuses in Indiana and Montana. In Texas this is not new. It's claimed that a well pad was installed just 400 feet away from a day-care centre at its Arlington campus.

More recently, the University of Tennessee wants to lease a portion of its 8,000 acre Cumberland Research Forest to frackers.

The University says it will use the revenue from the leases to fund studies into the environmental impact of fracking. Rushing into fracking and then evaluating the consequences and deciding later whether it was a good idea is hardly a type of judgement you would hope an academic body would recommend to its students. And it shows scant disregard for the precautionary principle.

Approaching the unbelievable is the case of Le Roy Middle and High School in Western New York, which actually had six wells drilled on school grounds. CNN news reported in February 2012 that it had found documents confirming that in summer 2011 a spill incident, or "violation", released liquid from two of the wells onto the ground, killing trees and vegetation where students play and practise sports. The report was triggered by the fact that since these incidents, no less than 18 female students at the school were diagnosed as suffering from a disease with symptoms similar to Tourette's Syndrome. CNN's reporter had taken the information on the drilling activities to experts, who confirmed the operation was fracking. The school was naturally reticent to comment, and had never reported the violations to parents. In response to the story the suggestion was put forward that the children's problem was Conversion Disorder, i.e. a psychiatric disorder rather than having a neurological cause. The issue divided the community. Another theory came forward, Pandas syndrome, a neurological disease caused by streptococcus. Antibiotic treatment improved the condition of some of the girls and the issue quietened down. Two new patients were reported in August 2012, but no evidence of contamination was found or admitted by the school authorities. The case remains to some an unsolved mystery, to others unmysterious, an example of mass hysteria. In any event it will remain a historical reminder of how fracking, or concern about fracking, may have unsuspected indirect health consequences. And how unwise was a school which allowed fracking on its premises.

In Texas and in Colorado wells have encroached on residential areas and school grounds. One can only hope such examples of industry greed could not happen in the UK.

There are signs that in the US action is being taken. In January 2013 a New York Times blog tells us that a team of toxicologists from the University of Pennsylvania is leading a national effort to study the health effects of fracking. The University's Center of Excellence in Environmental Toxicology is working with researchers from Columbia and the University of North Carolina to investigate and analyse reports of fracking-related symptoms - nausea, headaches, breathing difficulties and other ills from people who live near natural gas drilling sites, compressor stations or wastewater pits, with the aim of bringing academic discipline to the national debate.

"The Marcellus Shale is a microcosm of what's going on across the globe," Dr.Trevor Penning, head of the Penn group said. Let us wish him luck. With a strongly pro-industry Republican Governor and Republican-led state legislature which have denied funding to health studies on fracking, he will need it.

If frackers deny that their "normal" activities pollute, they can not deny that the growing list of "fraccidents" across the US are evidence that the industry is far from perfect in its practical operation.

Just a few examples - chosen to illustrate the spread of event type:

North Dakota July 2011: a spillage of an estimated 2 million gallons of brine.

Michigan February 2011: the state's first reported leak, just 1000 feet down.

Wyoming August 2006: a well blow-out which vented an estimated 4 million cubic feet of gas into the air, causing local residents' evacuation and contaminating drinking water.

Wyoming July 2008: tests revealed well water contaminated in 88 of 220 wells, containing benzene at 1500 "safe" levels.

Colorado June 2012: an employee killed working at a BP compressor station (needed to pressurise gas to make it flow along pipelines). 2 others injured by the explosion. The plant was shut down.

Oklahoma January 2012: a drilling rig hit an unexpected shallow gas pocket causing an explosion and fire.

Louisiana 2009: 16 cattle found dead near a drilling rig, apparently after drinking an unknown fluid.

Louisiana April 2010: hundreds of people evacuated after a well blow-out contaminated a drinking water aquifer.

Texas April 2011: escaping gas triggered a gas well explosion burning five acres of the surrounding state-owned park.

Texas January 2012: a fire at a wastewater disposal well injured three people after an oil tank exploded.

Ohio December 2007: a home exploded when methane entered nearby water wells and the basement of the home.

West Virginia September 2009: nearly all aquatic life was wiped out from a 30 mile stretch of the Dunkard Creek reportedly due to toxic algae resulting from wastewater discharge.

Pennsylvania December 2009: whilst boring a path for a pipeline 13 feet under a stream and wetland, between 3000 and 6000 gallons of synthetic drilling mud spilled into the wetland and reached the stream.

Virginia September 2008: a natural gas pipeline exploded destroying two homes and injuring five people.

Pennsylvania March 2010: an impoundment filled with wastewater exploded. Residents reported strong odours in the days before the explosion and a fire which shot flames a hundred feet high with a black plume of smoke visible for miles.

Pennsylvania March 2009: a pipeline transporting wastewater to an impoundment pit sprung a leak sending about 5000 gallons of waste into a watercourse.

Pennsylvania September 2008: a gas well explosion resulted in a fire which burned for two weeks.

Pennsylvania February 2009: 295 gallons of hydrochloric spilled at a drill site. In March 2009: 420 gallons spilled into a pond and caused a dead vegetation zone. (UK might note that hydrochloric acid is one of the chemicals that Cuadrilla claims is harmless).

Pennsylvania January 2011: a blow-out spewed some 21,000 gallons of sand and fracking fluid onto the surrounding land.

Pennsylvania January 2010: a haulage company was fined for spilling 7 tons of waste sludge along a road.

Pennsylvania 2009: residents were evacuated after a well casing failed and methane seeped into an adjacent abandoned well, blowing out its casing and travelling a third of a mile underground.

Pennsylvania December 2007: a CBM well exploded killing one worker and seriously injuring another.

Pennsylvania: a new well fracking forced gas into old gas wells nearby which then percolated up through water and mud to surface near homes.

Pennsylvania October 2008: the levels of dissolved solids in a 70 mile stretch of the Monongahela river, a source of drink water for over 700,000 people, were found above government standard levels. The area's tap water had an earthy taste and smell and left a white film on dishes. Used fracking fluids are sent to plants which discharge the water after treatments into the Monongahela.

The above could be supplemented, in particular, by numerous examples of water contamination. In Pennsylvania the contamination of water wells is so common that in 2006 the state appointed a full-time inspector dedicated to the issue.

The latest event recorded as this book is in production, is the death of a worker on the 15th February 2013 in an explosion at a fracking pad in West Virginia.

Since methane evaporates out of drinking water it is not considered "toxic" in the strict sense of the word. Which is why people like Cuadrilla's Francis Egan can attempt to deceive us by saying his product is not harmful.

However, the presence of methane in water supplies can be an indicator of gas wells linking with water systems. In Pennsylvania's case it is thought that much methane seepage comes from the thousands of old wells, but a 2004 disaster which killed three people and incidents in 2009 were linked to problems with newly drilled and active wells.

Another example of attempted deception comes from reports of one of the latest incidents, on 11th February 2013. This was a spill of an unknown amount of fracking waste from a fracking well at Windsor, Colorado. Greenish-brown flow-back fluid and steam were spewing from the well for nearly 30 hours. The wellhead had suffered a mechanical failure on the surface. Repairs were expected to take weeks. Bart Brookman, a senior vice-president of PDC Energy, the company in charge of the well, was at pains to deny the "fraccident" was fracking related. He said, in a typical industry move to separate the act of fracking from the whole operation, "Trying to associate this incident with fracking is not fair."

A spokesman from Windsor-Severance Fire Rescue saw it differently. This situation was different from conventional gas wells they were used to handling.

"I don't recall ever having a situation like this in all the natural gas wells we have," said Vess, who has been with the department for 12 years and worked in Windsor for nearly 20 years, according to newspaper Windsor Now, the local news service.

As anti-fracking web page Refracktion put it:

"When something goes wrong "fracking" gets defined very narrowly by the industry as the particular act of hydraulic fracturing not the end to end process of extracting gas using the process. The public don't have time for such weasel words. We are concerned about the reality."

The voices of those affected by fracking are now being raised in numerous ways, and the role of the Internet in pulling people together to share experiences and realise they are not alone is considerable. The Pennsylvania Alliance for Clean Water and Air has produced and regularly updates a list of those claiming to have been damaged by fracking - a List of the Harmed.

At the time of writing, February 2013, this lists over 800 individuals and families. Along with each is a brief citation of location, well operator, type of exposure and complaint, with further reference where more detail is to be found. Health symptoms range from constant anxiety through a mixture of diseases ranging from headaches and nausea to cancer, to deaths. Problems with pets and livestock, and loss of property value also figure in the list, with lawsuits including class actions outstanding in some cases. And of course many instances of polluted water.

But according to Leon Jennings, remember, in the UK we should trust in Cuadrilla.

"There's been millions of fracks performed worldwide, successfully, safely, and environmentally friendly."

Transparently deceptive, Jennings really is no asset to his company.

9 Finding a voice

Up against administrations both at federal and state level which pursued blindly the perceived economic benefits of fracking, and facing an industry with enormous financial and lobbying power, it is not surprising that the concerns about fracking went unheeded for so long in the US. And it is maybe no wonder that individuals who felt they had suffered from the industry's operations also felt impotent.

That is changing, but a feeling is still there of frustration and hopelessness.

It is worth reading in full the heartfelt gratitude and encouragement that one Pennsylvania resident wrote in response to a visit by celebrities to her Pennsylvania town.

In 2012 the organisation Artists Against Fracking was founded. The artists included high-profile stars such as Lady Gaga. And most potentially influential of all, Yoko Ono and Sean Lennon. The artists of this lobbying organisation came together over concerns about the impacts of fracking on water, air and local communities in the State of New York, which remains their first priority.

It would be easy for a cynical industry to dismiss such a grouping as irrelevant, and retreat to its stance claiming itself to be well-regulated and safe. But they would be unwise to do this, as they themselves recognise.

Another high-profile media event came in late 2012, the launch of the US fiction film "Promised Land". Before anyone had seen the film, in April 2012, it became the object of fierce debate. The star, Matt Damon, was accused by the industry of producing an anti-fracking movie. A pro-fracking PR campaign was mounted, with plans by industry hacks to send "scientific" studies to film critics, to distribute leaflets and to use social media to attack the film.

The industry had been active in pillorying "Gasland", but the new film produced a new rage, perhaps because being a work of fiction it was less open to direct attack. The film was smeared because of its funding, which included a contribution from the oil-producing country Abu Dhabi.

Maybe the industry now realises it overreacted, as the film's limited critical acclaim and its takings have so far not shown it to be a big success.

This hasn't stopped the production and extensive promotion by the industry of a pro-fracking film Fracknation. This documentary purports to address "unfounded" concerns about fracking which the industry claims are based on misinformation. Although its main target was Gasland, the timing of the film's premiere followed soon after the release of "Promised Land" and the major release is to coincide with the full theatrical release of "Promised Land".

The funding of Frackland was manipulated by a huge industry-inspired launch on Kickstarter to achieve public funding. The fundraising target was a mere $150,000.

The episode illustrates how the industry has recognised the rise of opinion against it, which should be some consolation to the anti-fracking movement.

On the 17th January 2013, Artists Against Fracking co-founders Yoko Ono and Sean Lennon, along with Susan Sarandon, Arun Gandhi, Josh Fox and other activists, plus the press, went on a tour of fracking sites in Susquehanna County, Pennsylvania.

Yoko Ono reported her distress at seeing the operation up close for the first time, and realising how the local landscape was impacted. But that for her was less heartbreaking than meeting victims of fracking, and being invited into their homes to hear their stories.

She asks the questions many have been asking. Especially those of us from outside the USA.

"Why is this national tragedy being kept quiet? Why aren't any politicians doing anything about it?"

If the visit made Yoko Ono cry, it was a symbol of hope to the people she met.

Rebecca Roter of Kingsley reported to Artists Against Fracking and on social media her thoughts from the heart, which are worth repeating in full.

"Yoko Ono, Sean Lennon, Susan Sarandon, and Arun Gandhi accomplished more in one day to draw national attention to the human cost of shale gas extraction than our collective voices have in six years of confronting natural gas development in Susquehanna County. Local news reports about the celebrities' tour of Susquehanna County gasfields finally included the voices and personal stories of local residents speaking about the human cost of shale extraction as they have experienced it. The press had to cover that story because the celebrities about whom they thronged were listening to us – to Tammy and Matt Manning, to Ray Kemble, to Victoria Switzer, to Vera Scroggins, to Craig Stevens, to Brett Jennings, to Frank Finan, to Josh Fox, to myself.

"The celebrities had come here on a bus to hear the voices that have been marginalized by media, by industry spin, by the state of Pennsylvania. They did not come for a sound bite or to take a photograph of flaming tap water – they wanted to reach out to us, to the people living with fracking, and to see for themselves how our lives have been affected by shale gas extraction.

"They experienced being followed by industry people while witnessing well pads. They got a taste of what it is like to stand witness to the truth of the gasfields as an industry worker yelled and shouted at them about jobs. They brought us hope and validation by simply coming to see what our new normal is like as we live in industrial gas fields and infrastructure, by reaching out to hear our voices. I am very grateful to all of them for seeking the truth, for hearing our voices with compassion, for keeping the issue of fracking mainstream on the heels of Matt Damon and John Krasinski's "Promised Land."

"As people with celebrity status focus on the real environmental and societal costs of fracking, it brings these issues into mainstream consciousness and keeps the national dialogue alive. The natural gas industry wants to manage public outrage over the harm that fracking does to water, to air, to human health, so the last thing they want are human interest stories from American gasfields.

"Yoko Ono, Sean Lennon, Susan Sarandon, and Arun Gandhi came to Susquehanna County offering compassion, offering their voices and their celebrity status to help communicate just how badly our water, our air,

our health, our entire environment is being impacted by shale gas extraction. They get that we need to come together, to cross over county and state lines to stand together to save our water, our air, our health, our America from a corporate energy development plan where profit is the bottom line. They get it – we need to come together internationally to stop fracking.

"Two days after the bus tour, I went to a Savoy Brown blues concert in Jim Thorpe PA, ninety miles from my home in Susquehanna County. Knowing the Marcellus is under Jim Thorpe, I asked the bartender as she handed me a glass of red wine if people had signed natural gas leases in the area. She looked at me and said, "Fracking? Yoko Ono is talking about fracking. That's how I found out about it."

10 Skittle alley - gas prices

It's time to look at the pro-fracking arguments that are mustered in the UK. I think we can knock them down one by one without too much difficulty.

The prime argument is that in the UK shale gas will provide an energy miracle which will not only reduce the price of gas but benefit our economy. This quotes the US experience with the suggestion we should believe it can happen here.

Next comes the claim that shale gas will increase our "energy security". This feeds both xenophobes and those who believe the scare story that if we don't do something about energy the "lights will go out".

Thirdly comes the argument that shale gas is a clean resource. It is a quick solution to cutting carbon emissions. The assumption is that it is impossible to move to genuine low- or non- carbon fuels in the near future. Shale gas is therefore billed as an ideal "transitional" fuel.

Is shale gas the "magic bullet" or "game changer" fracking advocates proclaim it to be?

Now they have realised there is an educated public alerted to the dangers of fracking, senior politicians, at least, are wary of repeating the claim that the UK can follow the US example and that shale gas fracking here can bring gas prices down to the extent that consumers will see energy price reductions. This is a myth for several reasons.

Firstly, in the US fracking was given its head when few people realised the dangers. In the absence of firm regulation shale gas companies were able to reduce costs and cut corners. This is no longer entirely the case in the US and it will not be the case in the UK. The frackers, indeed, were victims of their own success, and reduced gas prices to uneconomic levels, which is why after bottoming out prices are on the rise again. And which is why some fields are creating environmental mayhem by flaring gas without value. And why companies are looking to more naif markets where the gas price regime is such that they can increase their company profits.

Various bodies - not just environmentalists - have come on board recently to counter the claim that shale gas can be a "game changer" in the UK.

In January 2013 Sam Laidlaw, chief executive of British Gas owner Centrica told the Telegraph that it would be at least a decade before the UK saw any shale gas production and even then it would not be the game changer seen in North America.

He went on to say that other obstacles to shale success included planning regulations, population density, and landowners' rights.

In the US, in the majority of cases landowners have owned the rights to gas below their land and have been able to make substantial amounts - often millions - from leasing their land for fracking.

This is not the case in the UK. All rights to oil or gas below ground belong to the state. Landowners merely retain access rights.

This has led commentators to suggest the industry will find it difficult to persuade landowners to part with their rights for a fraction of what American landowners have achieved.

This omits consideration of two facts. Firstly that if the government, rather than individual landowners, owns mineral rights (and hence revenue) then if the industry secures government support this actually makes life simpler for the frackers. Especially when individual landowners have no veto over access to their land. If the government decides that fracking is in an overriding national interest then individual landowners will find it difficult or impossible to object successfully to frackers gaining access to their land without establishing a full and reasonable cause.

If fracking goes ahead we can expect to see legal challenges in future, and delays to fracking plans caused by court delays. However, I would suggest that if individual landowners refuse access to their land the fracking companies will simply side-step them and find someone else willing to take their money.

I have already indicated that the obstacles of planning regulations can be overcome by government running rough-shod over local opposition, but the population density problem remains a good argument against fracking in Britain.

The UK has a population far denser than the US. We are a small country and even our rural areas are highly populated compared with large areas of the US, and indeed with some areas of other European countries such as France or Italy

The ECCC took note of this - they said:

"Another barrier to shale gas development in the UK is the population density. For example, England has a population density of 383 per sq km, whereas the US has a population density of 27 per sq km."

The Geological Society told the committee that onshore footprints were high compared with conventional hydrocarbons. Cuadrilla, however, said that drilling up to 16 wells from a single pad would significantly reduce visual impact. Shell agreed. This, of course, ignores the fact that multiple well pads are already a standard practice in the US. And that our "rural" areas are not only in scarce supply compared with the US, but mostly in use for agriculture.

A look at how up to 80 pads could be spaced in a small area such as the Fylde shows that almost *all* of an important agricultural area would have shale gas horizontal drillings under its surface.

Lancashire County Council say:

"The most productive land in Lancashire is concentrated in the west of the county (mostly in the Fylde and West Lancashire) where much is classified by DEFRA as top grades 1 and 2, capable of growing a very wide range of agricultural and horticultural crops. Indeed, these areas represent the largest concentration of top quality farmland in the west of Britain."

Yet these are precisely the rural areas which Cuadrilla have picked on to drill under.

According to one of the EU's September 2012 reports, surface installations for multiple well pads require an area of approximately 3.6 hectares per pad for high volume hydraulic fracturing during the fracturing and completion phases. This was by reference to both the New York State DEC estimate and that of

Nature Conservancy, who estimated that 3.6 hectares of forest land would be taken per well pad, including roads and other infrastructure.

Yet Cuadrilla says its pads will only be about the size of a football field. An average football pitch in the UK is around 0.7 hectares. There is a discrepancy here. It seems that Cuadrilla are leaving out large areas they do not consider as being part of a well pad, or maybe they are attempting to avoid environmental regulation which requires environmental impact statements to be prepared for applications of under one hectare.

Rural areas in the UK are not well-provided for in terms of roads. Nor would some people like to see an increase in roads and traffic in these areas. The European Union's environment committee looked at environmental aspects of shale gas fracking, and in its risk assessment report said that in New York state it was estimated that a total of 7,000 to 11,000 truck movements would be generated per 10-well pad. And the resulting impacts would include noise, visual impact, air emissions in addition to infrastructure damage, congestion and road safety. Cumulative impacts would become serious if site separation was approximately 1.5km. This site separation is what Cuadrilla would need in the Fylde to reach its suggested required number of wells and pads.

A point omitted in the traffic review is the infrastructure or visual impact of conveying the gas to electricity-producing plants, the traffic and other disruption caused by installing pipelines, or alternatively the need for extensive cabling to transmit electricity if produced on-site.

In addition to the hurdles in planning terms of industrialising rural areas and taking agricultural land out of production, the industry is bound to generate significant local opposition. The various factors will inevitably combine to interfere with the industry's timescales as well as its production costs.

If shale gas exploiters will have to take measures to overcome the limitations of operating in fairly densely populated rural areas, then it seems clear that the costs to the industry of shale gas extraction would be higher than in the US. For this single reason alone, in the UK we could *never* have cheap gas in the UK, as they do in the US.

But we don't even have similar vehicle petrol and diesel prices to the US. At the end of January 2013 the price of petrol in the US was around $3.54 per gallon, equivalent to around £0.59 per litre. For diesel $4.22 = $0.67/l. In the UK at the same time prices averaged here, according to the AA, £1.32 for a litre of petrol and £1.40 for diesel.

This is a huge difference which is not explained by oil prices. It is largely dependent on difference of tax regimes, which is another reason shale gas prices would never have the impact they have had in the US. The UK government is neither going to give away its income from its ownership of our gas rights, nor reduce taxes.

The link between oil and gas prices, which impacts Europe more than the US, will reduce the impact of shale gas's ability to bring prices down. In any event, even Cuadrilla's hopes for shale gas in the UK are restricted to providing a quarter of our gas needs over a timescale of forty years, and with a lead time of some twenty years. These hopes are probably optimistic and based on today's gas requirement rather than any future rising demand.

In fact few politicians, outside the cartel of Osborne, Cameron and Hayes, are now claiming that shale gas will bring prices down. Because it won't.

Pro-frackers may rightly point to concerns about the rising costs of energy, particularly domestic bills which impact particularly on the elderly in winter. But their analysis of cause and remedy is wrong.

Shale is not the answer to fuel poverty. And gas prices are not directly related to production costs. There are many forces at work to keep domestic consumer prices high.

More benefit to the economy - and to the environment - would arrive by the government adopting energy scenarios based on green action. Energy efficiency, elimination of unnecessary waste, home improvement and insulation - these measures could make a difference for all the UK's population, not just the poor and the elderly. So would targeted tax action. In reality the government is pursuing counter-productive measures.

The main hope of the more realistic pro-shale advocates is that shale gas may help in preventing further damaging price rises for consumers.

Energy Secretary Ed Davey was quoted in December 2012 as having severe reservations about shale gas impact on prices.

"Some people though have looked at North America and are very excited that if we go for shale gas then we'll get cheaper energy," he told Sky News.

"I'm afraid I wish I could (say) we would definitely have cheaper energy as a result of this but I can't say that.

"First of all we don't know whether we will find lots of technically recoverable shale gas in the United Kingdom and the chances that it will affect our gas price I think, most experts think, is unlikely."

Even pro-fracking John Hayes admitted to the ECCC in January 2013, when speaking to knowledgeable MPs rather than an assumed ignorant media and electorate:

"Predicting gas prices is an inexact science. If you look at some of the predictions for gas prices, historically, they have not been followed by the events they anticipated. Nevertheless, notwithstanding the different scenarios, the likely impact from widespread exploitation of shale needs to be measured against the consensus of forecasts, which suggest that the gas price will continue to be tight. That is not least because demand for energy is growing rapidly in emerging economies and elsewhere. I do not want to get into the realms of fiction, still less fantasy, but it may be that China or another large, growing, emerging economy starts to invest in unconventional gas. That is not something that we could anticipate in our considerations here with any certainty or confidence. The consensus view is that the gas price is going to be tight, although you are absolutely right that shale locally could have significant impact."

What he means by "tight" is at best stable, and that gas prices are not going to come down.

Pro-frackers should also turn their attention to just why energy bills have increased. Here's one reason. In February 2013 the Guardian reported that Britain was exporting gas to the continent at a lower price than it was importing it, giving rise to fears that household bills are being inflated. It said that market distortion was worst in the coldest months, when the demand for gas is greatest, when "flows against price difference" (FAPD) took place on three out of four days. Between October and December 2011, the UK imported large volumes of Qatari gas despite it being up to 5% more expensive than gas exported to the continent.

Between December 2011 and October 2012 the UK exported 15 times more gas through the interconnector between UK and Belgium than it imported.

Caroline Flint, the shadow energy secretary, said:

"Energy companies always blame wholesale gas costs on price rises, so people will not understand why we appear to be exporting cheap gas and importing expensive gas.

"For too long, these energy companies have been allowed to get away with running their businesses in such a complicated way that it is almost impossible for anyone to know what the true cost of energy is."

Greenpeace's Leila Dean was blunter in her response to the report:

"The gas market has once again been revealed as a dark and murky world. George Osborne's dash for gas won't lower bills – it'll leave consumers even more open to exploitation."

Even the pro-frackers are cautious if you read what they actually say rather than what press headlines imply they say.

After the announcement of the new incentives for shale gas George Osborne said:

"America's success in unconventional gas is giving them low energy costs and cutting their carbon at the same time," he said. "We don't want British businesses and families to be left behind as gas prices tumble on the other side of the Atlantic."

He doesn't say that we will see gas prices tumble. But there is the sly impression that they could.

David Cameron said in a hearing on 11th December 2012:

"It would be a big risk just to ignore what is happening in the gas market," he said. "If we ignored it completely, you could be giving your economy much higher energy prices than is necessary."

Which is different from saying gas prices could come down.

However a No 10 spokesperson was less guarded, showing how much Cameron wants to push fracking:

"There's great potential for prices to come down That's something that's attractive about finding another source of energy".

Ed Davey was no doubt aware that a number of industry commentators and consultants had looked at shale gas and were doubtful about claims that had been made for it.

In late December 2012 consultancy Wood Mackenzie produced perhaps the least optimistic view. They went to the lengths of saying that for shale gas to be commercially viable in the UK it required a spot price of $9.68 per million btu, considerably more than 2012's average of $8.69 and the $8.5 that Bloomberg forecast as an average between 2015 and 2020.

Not only were they pessimistic about the viability, but they declared it premature for any estimates of the ultimate impact on UK gas supply because of the lack of knowledge of the recoverable volume of gas in the UK.

Yvonne Telford, a Wood Mackenzie analyst, told the Independent: *"We think it is unlikely that shale gas from the UK alone will have a material impact on the UK's gas price dynamics to 2025."*

Jim Watson, professor at the University of Sussex, told the Guardian and repeated the message widely in other media: *"Even if UK shale gas resources turn out to be large and low-cost – and that is a big if – this will not necessarily bring down prices to UK consumers. It is unlikely that UK shale gas will be anywhere near as cheap as it is in the US, and any price difference between UK gas and continental European gas will quickly disappear as a result of demand from other countries."*

In October 2012, Dr Neil Bentley, of the CBI (Confederation of British Industry) said:

"Energy investment is as much about growth as it is about secure, low-carbon power."

This comment hints at the CBI's main priority - economic growth. But despite the fact that the CBI support shale gas development for this reason Dr Bentley went on to say:

"All the evidence points towards a balanced and diverse energy mix as the most cost effective pathway to decarbonisation. This includes new nuclear, new renewables, new carbon capture and storage and new gas.

"The Government is right to encourage safe shale gas extraction as it makes sense to maximise the amount of energy we can produce at home at a reasonable cost. But gas alone isn't the answer.

"Most modelling shows future European gas prices rising, with or without an influx of unconventional gas, and so from both a cost and a security perspective, a mixed portfolio of generating technologies looks favourable.

"So let's stop arguing over the energy mix and focus on attracting investment to create jobs and growth as quickly as possible."

Whilst the CBI remains committed to shale gas, the comment about prices is significant. The CBI does not believe that shale gas will bring low gas prices.

Evidence mounts by the week that there is no confidence in the UK shale gas market. Bloomberg New Energy Finance said in a February 22nd 2013 report that the UK's efforts to build a shale gas industry would fail (not that they might fail or were likely to fail but that they *would* fail) to deliver a decline in prices as the cost would be too high and the output too slow. How many more warnings does it take that predictions it will lower prices are just "wishful thinking", as BNEF say?

Gas pricing is a complicated issue, especially when we work up from wholesale gas pricing to what the consumer pays. But even if – and it's a big if - fracking were successful in bringing in shale gas at an economic price, this would not significantly affect wholesale gas prices. In the UK gas is traded like other commodities – by on the spot market trading, by forward and futures trading (ie gambling) and under off-market contracts, where normal market mechanisms don't apply. Daily spot prices balance supply and demand BUT the UK is linked in to the European market, and we do not have market independence. We have pipelines linking us in to Europe on a two-way transfer and agreement basis, meaning that any UK supply increases would spread the impact across Europe and not be confined to benefitting the UK. And an important feature of the European market is the link to oil prices.

At present, wholesale gas prices are significantly higher than supply costs.

Taken together, all the factors mean any benefits to consumers of shale gas would be negligible. The only benefit of any conceivable lower production costs would be increased profits for the gas companies.

11 Skittle alley - the economy

Despite its doubts regarding gas prices, the CBI has bought the argument that shale gas would boost the economy. Have they been conned?

Cuadrilla repeat on their website earlier press release material stating that a study they had commissioned and published in September 2011 (by Regeneris) concluded that Cuadrilla could provide 5,600 jobs in the UK, and of these 1,700 would be in Lancashire. Ultimately this was derived from Cuadrilla's estimate of 200 trillion cubic feet of gas in place (GIS) in the Lancashire Bowland Shale. They were optimistic that if a fraction of this could be extracted there was "every chance" that Cuadrilla could give Lancashire a major boost in investment and jobs.

Needless to say, if the estimates of shale gas in place are guesswork, so are any resulting estimates of job creation, although Cuadrilla have been using a 20% rule-of-thumb for extraction potential.

Mike Hill, a Chartered Engineer who lives in the Fylde, has suggested that in reality lower figures of 1 to 5% are more probable, and that to achieve more than 10% would require drilling more wells than Cuadrilla have forecast.

The uncertainty about Cuadrilla's estimates did not prevent others from embellishing these figures. In an interview with the Independent, repeated in the Telegraph, former BP chief executive Lord Browne and Cuadrilla director said Lancashire could become the capital of Europe's shale gas industry and fracking could create up to 50,000 UK jobs.

How Lord Browne conjured up these figures, no doubt whispering them in the ears of the Cameron Osborne policy powerhouse, is unclear.

But by summer 2012 the figures quoted by Cuadrilla in a newsletter distributed to Fylde residents went back down to their previous levels, i.e. 5,600 nationwide.

Cuadrilla added:

"The production phase, if entered, is likely to last many decades, creating long term employment opportunities."

A look at the actual report which gave rise to Cuadrilla's claims, from consultants Regeneris, "Economic Impact of Shale Gas Exploration & Production in Lancashire and the UK", paints a different picture.

The report states that regarding the 5,600/1,700 median estimates *"this quantum of per-annum jobs maintained over an 11 year period from 2016 to 2026 inclusive"*.

After this period the Regeneris estimate of jobs drops to 200, although others with industry experience suggest this could realistically be reduced to 50.

Fylde MP Eric Ollerenshaw (Lancaster and Fleetwood, Conservative) said the following during a parliamentary debate on Shale Gas Profits on 19th December 2012:

"There is lots of talk about job creation, but as far as I can see, the thousands of jobs promised will not be created. As I understand the engineering process, once fracking wells are set up and the gas is being used, the jobs involved are support jobs. It is likely that the specialist engineers will be brought in from elsewhere."

In the US it is not only the case that "specialist engineers" are imported. Because of the short-term nature of the process, often lesser skilled personnel are imported to the local area. Cuadrilla boasts of offering training to local people, but if the jobs peter out after a decade or so, how will those who have been trained up have the opportunity to use those skills? Will they want to move to Cuadrilla's next adventure in Poland or the Ukraine?

The US experience raises other issues of mobile workforces being imposed on local communities. There are reports from fracking "boom towns" that crime has risen, particularly crime against women.

In Dickinson, North Dakota, there was a report of at least a 300% increase in assault and sex crimes over the past year. The mayor attributed the increase in crime to the oil and "natural" gas boom in their area.

The Executive Director of the Abuse & Rape Crisis Center in

Bradford County, Pennsylvania, Amy Miller, confirmed that there has been an increase in unknown assailant rapes since the gas industry moved into the region. Miller also noted that domestic abuse has spiked locally, with the cases primarily from gas industry families. The county has more than 700 wells drilled, with more than 300 of these operational, and another 2,000 drilling permits have been issued.

In February 2013 the New York Times took up the story. There had been an increase in crimes against women, including domestic and sexual assaults. The deputy state attorney of Mckenzie County complained that incoming workers did not respect the law or people of North Dakota. The male workers did not make the area their permanent home. Prostitutes took advantage of the male influx, and were said to "troll the bars".

Blackpool, the largest town in the Fylde, already has more than its fair share of crime, including drugs, and prostitution. The last thing the town needs is a boom bringing with it a large influx of workers as in the NYT report.

Fylde management consultant John Hobson comments that the figures quoted by Cuadrilla for local economic benefit are pitifully small, given that the tourism industry, which could be permanently blighted by fracking, already employs 17,000 people in the Fylde, Blackpool and the Wyre.

He has also turned his attention to the local economic benefits claimed by Cuadrilla based on experience rather than guesswork.

Cuadrilla carried out a geophysical survey in the Fylde in early 2012. The fact that this was carried out after their activities spawned earthquakes, rather than before, highlights problems with the whole process and responsibility between regulators and industry. We shall see more evidence of Cuadrilla's incompetence in looking at local experiences during this testing, but for now we'll examine the claims regarding the contribution they say the survey made to the local economy.

On 26th June 2012 Cuadrilla claimed in a "community newsletter" that the survey had contributed around £1.5 million to the local economy since March 2012. (They also in the same newsletter issued an apology for the "disturbance" they admitted their survey had caused). The then CEO Mark Miller put his signature to the newsletter.

At a public meeting in St Annes, Miller was asked how this figure of £1.5 million was arrived at. He talked about "hundreds" of foreign workers being paid subsistence expenses, in addition to employing a local crew of fifty people. He was asked to back up his claims. Eventually PPS, Cuadrilla's PR company, sent a reply. In their response the figure had climbed to £1.8 million (in fact a simple error meant that even their presented total of £1,825,000 didn't tally with the breakdown offered).

An analysis of Cuadrilla's figures, using Cuadrilla's own Regeneris report for methodology, plus the Treasury's "Green Book" (which details methodologies for measuring the economic impact of Government intervention), tax assumptions and generous savings and "multiplier effect" estimates, immediately reduced the benefit to the local economy from £600,000 to £156,000.

Similarly, the quoted figures for other expenses appeared to be overestimates. Cuadrilla refused to state whether their figures for local expenditure were inclusive or exclusive of VAT.

In the words of the analysis of Cuadrilla's figures:

"The main discrepancy comes from the fact that they seem to have forgotten to discount taxation, savings and out of area spend from the wages and land access fee figures, in line with their own economic benefit report methodology, when calculating the benefit to the local economy."

The conclusion was that Cuadrilla's claim of the geophysical survey benefit to the local economy was overstated by between £900,000 and £1,070,000.

If Cuadrilla can attempt to distort the figures on a single phase of their operation, this casts considerable doubt as to how far any estimate of theirs as to jobs or the economy can be trusted.

Mark Miller was asked at a meeting in Piper's Height Caravan Park to explain the discrepancies. He shrugged the question off, saying something along the lines of "So we may have got a few figures wrong – what's important is that we are creating *some* benefit".

However we might deplore Miller's attitude, some people would find some sympathy with the "anything is better than nothing" argument if there were no alternative. But of course there is.

The future of nuclear power in the UK is uncertain, rightly. But shale gas is not the only energy industry offering to create employment. In October 2012 Wales Online reported that a new deal with Hitachi could mean jobs for Wales. Welsh Secretary David Jones said the deal to build a new reactor at Wylfa, Anglesey, would mean 6,000 construction jobs and 1,000 long-term jobs.

"This Is Bristol" reported similar figures for a new Oldbury nuclear reactor.

Prime Minister David Cameron told the BBC the Hitachi deal was a major step for the UK.

But nuclear plans are, however, now in disarray. In February 2013 Cumbria rejected disposal of nuclear waste in its area. No other area has shown any interest in hosting such a facility. A few days after the Cumbria announcement, a new Public Accounts Committee report showed the cost of cleaning up the Sellafield nuclear waste site has now reached a staggering £67.5 billion, with no sign of when cost estimates will stop rising.

On the 4th of February Centrica pulled out of a new Hinkley Point reactor project, and two more at Sizewell, in the face of spiralling costs and delays. No proposed remaining nuclear plants involve British companies. EDF - a French company - is expected to lobby the government for a new major subsidy.

The enthusiasm for nuclear power decades ago is coming home to roost. We should take a lesson from this, and avoid building problems for the future by embracing another hazardous technology.

So if nuclear is unlikely to give us a jobs and economy boost, is there any energy alternative? Of course - investment in renewables.

The powerful oil and gas industry will take every opportunity to attack renewables. But it remains indisputable that fossil fuels are on their way out. The best attempts of the shale gas proponents can not hide this. In promoting the last gasp of fossil fuels they are doing immense harm. They are still funding the fossil fuel myth.

Solar power is not a contentious issue in the UK. Primarily, I suggest, because there is still the belief, based on outdated solar power technology, that there isn't sufficient sun in the UK.

In January 2013 scientists at EMPA, the Swiss Federal Laboratories for Materials Science and Technology, announced they had developed thin film solar cells on flexible polymer foil with a new record efficiency for converting sunlight into electricity. EMPA's team believe they have made a significant leap ahead towards making solar electricity affordable on a large industrial scale.

In the US solar energy development has been the recipient of substantial state subsidy. But this encouragement starts to fall apart when it is found that the US started imposing substantial tariffs penalising Chinese solar imports. The US is more interested in protecting its domestic market than technological advances. That may not be surprising, but such protectionism raises prices for the consumer, in the end. A president who promises clean green energy but pushes its price up for the consumer really hasn't got his green policy in order.

In the UK you could be forgiven for thinking that solar energy projects were more due to individual initiative than government's. And onshore wind energy has certainly been controversial.

Nevertheless, the BBC was able to report in April 2012 that the Renewable Energy Association with its consultants Innovas had found that the renewables industry contributed £12.5 billion to the UK economy annually, and that the European Commission had said that low-carbon generation and energy efficiency could contribute five million jobs across the EU by 2020.

In a period of supposed recession, the renewables industry grew by 11% between 2009/10 and 2010/11 compared with overall growth of 1.4%.

The report also calculated that renewables generated exports of just under £1.6bn in 2010/11, with wind technologies the biggest contributor.

In the same report it was stated that 64% of young adults (88% in Scotland) wanted renewables to provide the bulk of new generation capacity installed between 2012 and 2020. An Ipsos-Mori report suggested similar support for wind farms and backing for the minor level of UK wind power subsidy - a mere 2p per day per household.

On the 5th February 2013 DECC published a new report on public opinion. More than three-quarters of respondents (in line with DECC's previous surveys) supported the UK's use of renewables. Onshore wind - often claimed to be extremely unpopular - was supported by most respondents, the opposition amounted to a mere 13%.

Attitude towards energy saving was, however, casual, with less than a third saying they gave energy efficiency in the home much thought. Just under a third were "worried" about their energy bills, with 18% "very worried". Only 12% of those worried about energy costs were more worried about their energy bills than other costs of transport, food, and other domestic costs. Around 50% were very concerned about steep energy rises in the future. But few planned to take immediate measures like changing energy supplier to achieve cheaper bills.

The question must be asked - what is the UK waiting for? Why is there not the political will to move towards a prosperous green economic future?

As an example of the muddled thinking on wind energy and shale gas, on 24th January 2013 DECC reported that energy minister Ed Davey was to sign an agreement to import wind energy from Ireland. Irish Minister for Communications Energy & Natural

Resources, Pat Rabbitte, said that Ireland can generate more wind power than it consumes. Yet the frackers are pursuing shale gas extraction in Ireland just as hard as in the UK. And the UK is backing away from producing its own wind power by reducing subsidies. The energy world is a crazy world.

In 2009 a report for the EU's European Environment Agency concluded that Europe's raw wind energy potential is huge, and that projections suggest that it may be equivalent to almost 20 times energy demand in 2020. And that - technical achievability apart - economically competitive wind energy potential amounts to more than three times projected demand.

The Guardian reported on 4th February 2013 that over the previous three months wind farms produced more electricity than any other power source in Spain for the first time ever. With our enormous offshore as well as onshore wind power potential, the UK would be stupid to pursue shale gas as an alternative.

Solar power is still on the rise in Germany, where it currently accounts for around 5% of energy production. The target is for 10% by 2020 and at least 20% by 2030. Research is continuing into new and hybrid technologies which will be productive even in places which are not comparatively well-off for sunshine.

There is more future, more long-term energy security, and more economic benefits and job prospects in pursuing wind and other renewables rather than shale gas. Not to mention less environmental impact.

12 Skittle alley - transitional fuel & energy security

The question mark has already been placed against the claim that shale gas is cleaner than conventional natural gas, and in the short term its economic benefit is in doubt. This puts paid to any suggestion that it has a valid place as a "transitional fuel".

Kevin Anderson, from the Tyndall Centre for Climate Change Research has clear views on this, as he told the press in December 2012:

"Shale gas is the same as natural gas – it is a high-carbon fuel, with around 75% of its mass made of carbon. For the UK and other wealthy nations, shale gas cannot be a transition fuel to a low-carbon future. Anyone who says differently does not understand our explicit international commitments under the Copenhagen Accord, the Cancun Agreements – or, alternatively, is bad at maths."

Anderson continues by clarifying that existing carbon budgets give no room for extra fossil fuel burnings, and that shale gas is lower carbon than coal only if we don't still burn the coal, a point that was made in an earlier chapter. According to Anderson, even if carbon capture and storage were made to work with shale gas the emissions reductions would not be enough to meet the UK's international carbon commitments.

"In the UK and globally, we are now reaping the reward of a decade of hypocrisy and self-delusion on climate change. We pretend we are doing something ourselves, whilst blaming others for rising emissions.

"The truth is out – it is a tragedy of the commons par excellence – we are all to blame and we have left it too late for a technical fix. We are heading towards a global temperature rise of 4C to 6C this century; if we want to get off this trajectory, shale gas needs to stay in the ground and we, in the wealthy world, need to consume much less energy – now."

To my mind the climate change imperative overrules consideration of how much we are dependent on other nations for gas imports. If we devoted as much time and thought to how we can overcome our dependence on other nations for our food security this would be well-spent effort.

In a situation where in the UK we are only self-sufficient in food to the extent of some 60%, we really have to question whether we should turn over good quality agricultural land to shale gas extraction.

But to address energy "security" it seems obvious that any home-grown energy can potentially reduce current dependence on foreign gas imports – either pipelined gas from Norway and the USSR or LNG from places like Qatar. But as we have already seen, in a complicated gas market this is not clear-cut. We export gas - and we export it at a lower price than we import it. This ludicrous situation hardly improves our "energy security".

Of course we are also dependent on coal imports and are currently dependent on coal supplies from Russia, Colombia and the USA. Ironically, the US shale gas success has resulted in increased imports of US coal. So much again for energy security. A cynic might think the attitude is that it's OK to import a polluting fuel from our political friends, but not from others.

At the end of the day, no-one knows how much shale gas there is under mainland UK, nor how much of it is extractable. In this situation it is foolish to even begin to think about how shale gas could change our dependence on energy from abroad. Except to comment if that if shale could even in the frackers' optimistic opinion provide around only a quarter of our gas "needs" and for a limited time period, then we are talking at best at around a tenth or less of our energy demand. Shale gas will not provide us with reliable future energy security.

Will the lights "go out"?

OFGEM, the Office of Gas and Electricity Markets, is a government regulator which has prime responsibility for monitoring the electricity and gas consumer markets. In essence it is charged with promoting competition within the UK between the electricity and gas companies. It has little or no competence outside that brief. However, OFGEM entered the shale gas argument when it commissioned a study which has been used by pro-frackers to advance their argument that there would arise a serious excess of UK energy demand over supply. The lights would "go out". The organisation OFGEM has come under serious criticism from the Labour Party. In October 2012 the Shadow energy secretary Caroline Flint told delegates at her party's conference that the time had come to axe OFGEM. It had "failed to get tough" with the energy giants. She presented policies that her party would introduce to reduce fuel bills, and establish a more trustworthy regulator.

OFGEM admits that its first Electricity Capacity Assessment, published in October 2012, was a one-off, outside its normal brief. Does it say we will have power blackouts in the UK? No. It asserts only that the oversupply of provision over demand - spare provision - is thought to reduce from 14% to 4% by 2015.

UKIP, climate change deniers to a man, have claimed that the country would have blackouts by 2020 due to closure of coal-fired power stations.

Greenpeace Director of Policy Doug Parr said "OFGEM warns again that relying on gas will leave the UK hooked on volatile imports and continue to push up household bills. The Government must act urgently to stop that happening."

Utilities Insider asked the question others might ask - maybe this report had been released to justify upcoming changes in shale gas policy.

Even pro-fracking Nick Grealy has not hidden his distrust of OFGEM and their consultants. He points to a report commissioned by them from Poyry and produced in July 2011 but which OFGEM did not issue until February 2012, by which time it was hopelessly out-of-date. Grealy describes Poyry as having "survived on the cash cow of DECC and OFGEM and banks for years" (a web article entitled "OFGEM's (ex?) favourite consultant on UK Shale Gas").

Green campaigners are sometimes accused of being scaremongers. But the pro-frackers who use the "Britain's lights will go out" argument and raise the spectre of old people dying in their droves if we don't embrace shale gas, are open to exactly the same accusation. And they are guilty.

The answer to the above question is this. The lights will not go out in 2015 or 2020 on any realistic scenario. If the government embarks on an active programme now of energy conservation, promotion of renewable energy, and a public education programme to instil the idea that we can not continue to use energy in the profligate way we have become used to, then we have a chance. We will have a long-term energy strategy which will carry us forward with clean energy and clean consciences into the next century. And by doing that we will have energy security.

At the end of January 2013 France's minister for ecology, sustainable development and energy Delphine Batho, announced that from 1st July 2013 shops and commercial enterprises would be obliged to switch off their lights at night.

It is expected that the move will save 2 Twh of energy per year, equivalent to the energy of 750,000 households, saving some 250,000 tonnes of CO_2 per annum.

13 Shale gas in the UK - fracking by stealth

Dr Richard Selley wrote in Marine and Petroleum Geology (2012) that the first shale gas experience in the UK was the result of drilling a well near Netherfield in West Sussex in 1875. A first exploratory well was abandoned for technical reasons after it reached around a thousand feet. A second reached 1905 feet through Kimmeridge Clay to Coral Rag. The clay was found to be naturally fractured. An injudicious exploration led to an explosion. No further exploration was attempted.

Despite efforts by Dr Selley and others, shale gas was not considered seriously in the UK until the US experience led to an interest when DECC produced a list of opportunities for oil and gas exploration - the "13th Round of Onshore Licensing" in 2008.

Licensing blocks covered some 64% of the England but the bids, and the licence grants, resulted in comparatively few take-ups, at least as far as an interest in shale gas was concerned.

But Cuadrilla Resources was granted PEDLs (Petroleum Exploration and Development Licences) in a number of blocks and the holding group now has the following licences and permissions (The additional names are Operator and Equity holder).

PEDL165 Bowland Resources Ltd
PEDL247, PL55 EXL189 Tanglewood Resources Ltd
EXL 269 Elswick Resources Ltd
PEDL244 Bolney Resources Ltd

PEDL165 is the one which will interest us most, as this is the block in Lancashire where Cuadrilla have put most of their exploratory effort. As noted earlier, Cuadrilla acquired the Elswick producing well in the same area.

PEDL247 and PEDL244 cover an area in Sussex including Balcombe, Bolney, Ashdown and Heathfield. Cuadrilla's interest centred on Balcombe, but they have met opposition and it is not clear how they will pursue operations in this area. EXL189 includes Cowden.

Other companies who come into the fracking picture have blocks in other areas. Coastal Oil and Gas Ltd, has interests in South Wales and Kent. It shares a parent company (UK Onshore Gas) with UK Methane Ltd, who also have interests in South Wales, plus Somerset. These are essentially the same business, a small venture with few resources which has speculated on the purchase of PEDL licences.

Dart Energy (Europe) Ltd, an Australian-held company, has a number of interests in Scotland, Wales, Cheshire, Yorkshire and the North East. Their prime target to-date has been Coal Bed Methane extraction CBM.

Island Gas (IGas) Ltd has interests in the North West and the Midlands, Greenpark Energy (!) has PEDLs in Staffordshire, Cheshire, Yorkshire and Scotland, and is targeting CBM. Fairfax Shelfco 320 Ltd holds a PEDL in Somerset and is possibly now owned by an American company AED.

As Nick Grealy said, Cuadrilla were really ahead of the field at the time in seeing shale gas potential. DECC are gearing up to putting a 14th round of exploration licences on offer. This is expected to include a proportion and distribution of blocks of the UK similar to what was on offer in the 13th round, but we can expect to see a lot more interest this time. The announcement of the opening period is still awaited. The issue of the 14th round was raised by Nigel Smith, Seismic/Basin Analyst from the British Geological Survey (BGS) ,who told MPs in November 2012:

"...we have had the 14th round of licensing delayed. If that had been enacted, lots of companies would have taken out licences, probably covering most of the country."

At the end of July 2009 Cuadrilla submitted an application to Lancashire County Council relating to Preese Hall Farm, Warton, for "Temporary change of use from agriculture to construction of a drilling platform upgrade of farm track and removal of hedges to create one of three passing places drilling of exploratory borehole and testing for hydrocarbons." This application was the first of five, and these successful applications may now have significant consequences for fracking in the Fylde. If you are not interested in the planning detail, feel free to skip to the summary at the end of this chapter. Planning applications involving minerals are made to the County Councils as mineral authorities, local councils (District or Borough and Parish Councils) only have rights to make their views known.

It seems amazing now, just a couple of years later, but in 2009 there was little or no public knowledge about fracking. The implications of these planning applications was not recognised. The Preese Hall application was decided by delegated powers. In other words, approval was given by an officer without the application going to councillor committee. The decision notice was dated 30th October.

Several individuals and organisations had been consulted on the application, including the appropriate county councillor Paul Hayhurst, the Environment Agency, Fylde Borough Council. landscaping, ecology and archaeology consultees, highways, National Grid Company PLC, United Utilities (water) Weeton and Preese Parish Council. The only detail response recorded on the LCC planning web site is from Fylde Borough Council. The letter is short.

"I refer to your recent consultation regarding the above development.

"The application has now been considered by this authority and I can advise you that the Fylde Borough Council raises no objections to the proposal."

No observations were received from Weeton-with-Preese Parish Council, nor from the Environment Agency.

The highways department made a minor comment, the National Grid Gas and National Grid Company, and the United Utilities had no objection.

Following advertisement of the application on a site notice and letters to neighbours, the only response recorded is from the Campaign to Protect Rural England, CPRE, who had no objection in principle but made a comment regarding adequate reinstatement.

The Director of Strategic Planning and Transport advised:

"Government policy is that it is in the national interest to ensure the recovery of all economic hydrocarbon reserves. An application to Central Government for a licence to drill will be submitted should planning permission be granted."

"The site is located on land designated as Countryside Area in the Fylde Local Plan. Policy SP2 states that development within Countryside Areas will not be permitted except where it is required for agriculture, horticulture or forestry or other uses appropriate to a rural area. The construction of a drilling platform is not one of the uses listed as appropriate in such areas but the operation would be of a temporary short term nature and has to be undertaken in this location in order to target a particular geological feature. The site is not in a prominent location being well screened by a mature woodland immediately to the east of the site. There would be distant views of the site from Poulton-le-Fylde but these would limited to the 36 metre high drilling rig mast. Provided that the land is restored upon cessation of the operations, it is considered that the proposal is acceptable in relation to Policy SP2 of the Fylde Borough Local Plan and Policies 7 and 106 of the Lancashire Minerals and Waste Local Plan."

In this statement we have the clear signpost to how seriously our planning protection has been undermined, and will continue to be undermined, by fracking interests.

The application was against rural policy, but this was secondary to considerations of "government policy".

Later in the game, the government mooted plans to take decisions on shale gas out of local authorities' control. But already, a few years earlier, LCC was voluntarily giving way to national pressure.

It is noted that the application makes no mention of hydraulic fracturing, only drilling a borehole. However, condition 15 of the decision notice required Cuadrilla to submit a borehole plan for approval, in order to protect water resources in the Sherwood Sandstone.

Cuadrilla were obliged, therefore to submit the measures they intended to implement, and did so in January 2010. This includes at last a very brief reference to well "stimulation".

This time the Environment Agency did reply to consultation requests. The response is short:

"Thank you for referring the above to us. We are satisfied that the information submitted is sufficient to discharge the above condition."

Jumping ahead for a moment to February 2013, Cuadrilla CEO Francis Egan said in a radio interview, after the resumption of fracking was announced:

"This is being done in a very staged and sensible fashion (I keep going back to it) we're going to drill one well and fracture two. There will be a one month log test, then we may move on to developing one site. Then from there perhaps two or three sites."

The tactics were clear from the 2009 planning application. Fracking the Fylde by stealth.

On the 3rd December 2009 Cuadrilla submitted an almost identical application to the Preese Hall one, this time for Hall Farm, Wharles. It was determined - again by delegated powers, in March 2010.

In early February 2010, Cuadrilla submitted a further planning application to LCC again for "Temporary change of use from agriculture to site for drilling an exploratory borehole and testing for hydrocarbons including construction of a drilling platform" and for highways access.

This Grange Road, Singleton application was determined on April 21st. This time the application went to committee, but the speed of the decision might indicate it did not receive lengthy consideration.

As a sop to the County Council's ecologist Alison Cox, and the Environment Agency who endorsed her view on this (their only comment on the application), the decision did include a condition that any floodlighting scheme should have an assessment of its impact on any bats that may forage at the boundary of the site. Suggestions for wider conditions from Ms Cox were ignored.

In July 2010 Cuadrilla put in their Becconsall, Banks application. This was decided on the 20th October - again by delegated authority.

This time there was more significant response.

Natural England is a non-departmental government body whose statutory purpose, in their own words, is to ensure that the natural environment is conserved, enhanced, and managed for the benefit of current and future generations, thereby contributing to sustainable development.

Personally I have never quite come to grips with what constitutes sustainable development.

However, Natural England said in their response to LCC in a letter of 13th August 2010:

"It is our opinion that the proposal may have a significant impact on the natural environment.

"Should the Local Authority decide that this proposal requires an EIA, we will be pleased to comment on the scoping report in due course."

"Should the Local Authority decide that this proposal does not require an EIA, we recommend that an Ecological Report and/or Landscape Report be prepared to support any planning application submitted."

It is not clear whether the application was ever "screened" by DCC as to the need for an EIA. Screening is the process by which a decision is taken for the need for an EIA. Scoping is the process by which the content and extent of an EIA is defined.

Rather curiously, LCC received a further letter from NE by email dated the 25th August - less than a fortnight later - giving a rather different response. This stated that in NE's opinion the proposed development would not materially or significantly the nearby Ribble Estuary Special Protection Area, a European site protected under the habitats regulations. (This is very close, one might say almost adjacent, to the proposed fracking site).

The NE letter went on to say the proposal did not have any significant impacts upon Natural England's "other interests".

The letter did, however consider that the Marsh Farm Fields Biological Heritage Site (BHS) could be affected and recommended consulting the county ecologist for his/her view.

The LCC ecologist Dr Sarah Manchester pointed out that the drilling site was within 1km of the Ribble and Alt SPA, and lies within Marsh Farm Fields Biological Heritage Site, which is important for its wintering wildfowl and wading birds.

Ms Manchester concluded that Cuadrilla's submitted ecological assessment (written by Ecology Services UK Ltd) was a reasonable evaluation. She made specific recommendations for planning conditions if LCC were minded to approve the application. These were that works that could affect nesting areas should be avoided between March and July, that no work should be carried out between October 31st and March 31st, and that no site development work should be carried out until a method statement had been prepared and agreed to avoid impact on the Marsh Farm BHS. She considered Ecology Services' recommendations for additional hedgerow, tree and shrub plantings, part of restoration proposals, as inappropriate.

Ms Manchester's recommendation on method statement was included as a condition of consent being granted.

This time the drilling site was within a different Borough council area, the West Lancashire Borough Council. Their consultation response was no objection. Sefton (metropolitan) Borough Council, had no objection subject to a comment on their involvement responsibility on highways. Hesketh-with-Becconsall Parish Council and North Meols Parish Council did not make any observations on the application.

No representations were made in response to advertisement in the press, site notice and neighbour notification.

The Council provided reasons for its decision as follows, worth quoting in full.

"The site is located on land designated as Coastal Zone in the West Lancashire Replacement Local Plan, where Policy EN3 applies. This

policy states that development within the Coastal Zone will be limited to that which is essential to meet the needs of coastal navigation, amenity and informal recreation, tourism and leisure, flood protection, fisheries, nature conservation and/ or agriculture. The application site also falls within the Marsh Farm Fields; North Meols Biological Heritage Site, which is designated for its value as a foraging area for wildfowl that use the nearby Ribble Estuary SSSI / SPA. The BHS designation is the subject of Policy EN1 of the West Lancashire Replacement Local Plan that seeks to restrict development to that required to meet an overriding local public need providing there are mitigation measures and compensatory habitat creation. The exploration operations are necessary to establish the extent of hydrocarbon reserves; it is Government policy to maximise the extraction of domestic energy supplies. The drilling operations have to be in this particular location to be able to target a particular geological feature. There is therefore a need to balance the need for investigations of this nature against the impacts the proposal may have on ecological and biodiversity interests."

In other words, the authority was bowing to government policy, and in doing so, disregarding its own policies and local interests.

Granting of permission was additionally prejudiced because a previous application by Archaean Energy (UK) Ltd for hydrocarbon drilling operations on this site had been approved in 2002 and renewed in 2005, although operations were not carried out. No objections had been raised to the 2002 application, although in that case North Meols Parish Council did ask that in the case of a "no find" the site be properly restored. West Lancashire Borough Council passed this on. The (LCC internal) ecology response said the proposal was acceptable in landscape terms but recommended that the Landscape Startegy should be borne in mind if a more permanent application were to be made in future.

Graham Harding, Director of the Environment Directorate, put his name to a notice to the public, inviting representations, stating *"The proposed development does not accord with the provisions of the development plan in force in the area in which the land to which the application relates is situated."*

The NFU reported concerns from one of its members - a grower of outside vegetable crops - to this application about dust and increased vehicular traffic along Bonny Barn Road. This member sent a letter to objection to LCC listing a number of other concerns.

A handwritten letter of objection in response to neighbour notification stated "I was very glad you asked for my families' opinion on the idea of drilling for hydrocarbons across the fields from our home. We are furious that someone should put short-term financial gain before concern for our environment."

Objections notwithstanding, the 2002 application was granted. The report to the committee described a history of exploration for oil and gas from the Fylde and West Lancashire extending into the Irish Sea. Again it emphasised the government's policy - to "seek the maximum exploitation of UK oil and gas reserves for reasons of security and supply and economic development".

Because Archaen Energy were unable to complete their operations in time, they applied for an extension, which was granted in 2005. Their reason for delay was that the weather had changed for the worse after the topsoil was stripped, and because of drilling rig availability. In addition they had had a change of MD. Archaen Energy requested voluntary dissolution in 2006 and was finally dissolved in April 2007. Archaen Energy's Land Manager handling the applications was Phil Mason. Mason was - and still is - the agent handling Cuadrilla's planning applications.

The Archean precedent highlights a number of issues regarding the planning system and its operation. The County Council was prepared to override its own development plan policies, and to disregard the importance of protecting its own biological heritage sites. It justified this by reference to the government policy on developing energy resources.

It was prepared to accept an application for "temporary" planning permission, in the knowledge that this could lead to a permanent application on the same site. Yet the council might (rightly perhaps) say that it could only consider the implications of the application actually before it.

More importantly, a "temporary" planning application will create a precedent for *any* future similar application on the same site. We can also forecast that the temporary permissions acquired in 2009-2010 will make it more difficult for future production applications to be refused, even if public awareness leads to sizeable public objection. Again this is fracking by stealth.

Cuadrilla's applications continued. In September 2010, the application was lodged for drilling at Anna's Road. It was granted by committee in November 2010.

The committee report again describes how "untemporary" this and the other temporary applications really are:

"If no gas is detected the borehole would be plugged and the site restored. If successful, the borehole would be temporarily sealed with a control valve and the rig and other temporary buildings would be removed. A further permission would then be sought for the retention of the platform and for any further testing or production facilities that may be required."

Fylde Borough Council had no objections. But the Parish Council, Westby-with-Plumptons, actually supported the application. No reasons were given, just the comment: "Parish Council supports the application."

The Environment Agency had no objection in principle, but the developer was to be "reminded" of a number of points covered by legislation. Two members of the public made representations, one concerned about traffic. This objection was acknowledged, but overruled as the disturbance would only be "temporary".

The site is within a proposed BHS, Lytham Moss (the decision conditions did require a plan for minimising disturbance of overwintering birds). The drilling operations would be undertaken for 24 hours, 7 days per week over a period of up to six weeks. The nearest residential property was only 250 metres away.

The prime reason for approval proposed to the committee was essentially that it was in the national interest. The report now says that this development *would* comply with the policies of the Development Plan. Listed in relevant policies is Fylde Borough Local plan policy SP2, which was stated in an earlier application as presuming against the development of drilling. I can see no logic here.

In summary, the planning applications submitted by Cuadrilla in 2009 and 2010 raise concern that the controlling authority Lancashire County Council was minded always to approve exploration drilling, in conflict with its own development policies, in what the officers perceived as an overriding national interest for energy source development. Granting of Cuadrilla's applications have established a precedent which can affect future exploration and development applications, despite the fact that when these applications were granted little was known about the potential consequences of fracking, on the part of the officers, the county councillors, the local councillors and the general public.

14 Shale gas in the UK - Work starts - and stops

When Cuadrilla started drilling at Preese Hall in August 2010, there was still little recognition and understanding of fracking. It wasn't until March 2011 that Cuadrilla announced to the ECCC that they had drilled down to about 9,200 feet, taking around 90 days to do so, and were preparing the Preese Hall well for fracturing, probably later that month. By then they had also drilled down to around 6,000 feet at Grange Hill. Later they announced that by July 2011 they had reached 10,700 feet.

Cuadrilla had also been active in the South of England from 2010. They had taken over an old gas well at Cowden in Kent, which was drilled by another operator in 1999, and it is possible that Cuadrilla carried out a test fracking. They themselves refer now to an "initial evaluation", after which they closed the site. They continue to say that they have no intention to carry out further work there.

In Sussex, Cuadrilla acquired the site of an old exploratory oil well, drilled by Conoco in 1986, and subsequently abandoned.

In January 2010 Cuadrilla submitted an application to West Sussex County Council for test fracking at Lower Stumble, just a mile south of the town of Balcombe. The agent was again Phil Mason. The application was to upgrade an existing stone platform and drill a borehole for oil and gas exploration. Again, as will be seen, Cuadrilla were using an old permission grant as leverage. Permission was granted in April.

What were the reasons for granting the planning permission? Firstly, there was an "identified need" for hydrocarbon exploration.

Mid Sussex District Council, as consultees, raised no objection (under delegated powers), subject to hoping it really was a temporary permission. The district ward members had made no comment. Natural England noted that the application was within an area of outstanding natural beauty (AONB) and urged the County to consider the application in this light. The proposal also had potential to adversely affect woodland classified in the Ancient Woodland inventory. The High Weald AONB Unit, with brief to protect the AONB, confirmed the site to be within the AONB, and this was contrary to Cuadrilla's supporting statement, which claimed "to the best of the applicant's knowledge" that the site was not part of an area with any statutory designation. This prompts the question of the competence of Cuadrilla's agent, if nothing else. No consultation response is recorded from Balcombe Parish Council. However according to an internet post on the "gasdrillinginbalcombe" opposition website, the application was approved by the Parish Council at a regular council meeting.

Cuadrilla made it clear that they saw fracking as part of the application, by describing it in their supporting documents (along with flaring of waste methane, a point lost on the County). Cuadrilla later attempted to contest this in a media statement of 9th December 2011 by saying they had no regulatory approval for fracking. This media fabrication came after a history of public disquiet about how Cuadrilla had been going about its business in Sussex. In October 2010 a media release by AJ Lucas confirming a then 25% stake in the prospect of shale gas in Bolney (i.e. Balcombe) clearly stated that after fracking Preese Hall and Grange Hill, Cuadrilla intended to frack at Balcombe. Once again Cuadrilla have been less than honest, or "open and transparent", putting it in their terms. Cuadrilla only failed in their plan for fracking Balcombe because their first frackings in Lancashire caused earthquakes and led to a freeze on the procedure.

There were two significant steps forward for fracking in 2011, the first being the release of the Select Committee's report in May and the government's response in July. I will cover this in more detail later, enough for now to say that the report was - rather misleadingly - regarded as the ECCC MPS giving the green light for fracking.

But the main event of 2011 came in Blackpool - the earthquakes. (It is tempting to wonder what would have been the Select Committee's reaction if these had occurred a couple of months earlier). The earthquakes effectively caused a stop to permissions being given to any other operators, although Cuadrilla's halt was described as a voluntary act. In any event there was a de facto moratorium, and fracking went on hold until the outcome of the investigations into the seismic events. It wasn't until April 2012 that a government-commissioned review into Cuadrilla's own report on their seismic effects (November 2011) was available for comment. And it took until December 2012 for the government finally to allow fracking to continue.

The eighteen months of lull in fracking gave the anti-fracking movement an opportunity to gather ground by leaps and bounds, prompted by the shock realisation that fracking caused earth tremors.

In August 2011 two men scaled half way up Blackpool Tower to erect banners protesting against fracking. They were held by police on suspicion of causing criminal damage and being on enclosed premises, and later released on bail having been charged with obstructing or disrupting a person engaged in lawful activity. The protesters were said by the press to be representing a web organisation, an interesting comment on the new power of the internet. The banners proclaimed "Fracking is coming to the UK" and "We can stop it. Frack-off.org". The protestors were described in the press as "a 24-year-old from East Sussex and a 63-year-old from Surrey", a pointer to the cross-country support the anti-fracking movement would attract.

Blackpool Tower workers were accused of risking the protesters' safety by using a pressure washer as the climbers dangled hundreds of feet above the ground.

The central message was this:

"The UK fracking industry is in its infancy. We must act now if we are to stop it in its tracks. It's bad for Lancashire, it's bad for the UK and it's bad for the planet."

Rob Basto, a doctor of physics and an experienced rock climber, clambered up Blackpool Tower with Robin Monaghan in the early hours of August 6. They used a mixture of free climbing and professional equipment to scale the structure and unfurl the banners before the police arrived.

Rob said "It's vital that people are able to highlight issues such as fracking that pose such a huge risk to the environment and society in general", and Robin, who was also convicted, confirmed the pair's commitment. "People in the Lancashire area should be seriously concerned. This is a completely unregulated corporate experiment. It is unacceptable and morally bankrupt that a private company can put something as sacred as people's health and our shared environment at risk in the search for short-term profits".

In November a further protest was mounted against Cuadrilla, this time at the rig site at Banks. "Around seven" (according to the Liverpool Echo report) protestors from Frack Off mounted an early morning entry to the site and six of these climbed onto the drilling rig, displaying a banner and putting a halt to operations.

Frack Off said the purpose of the action was to highlight the hypocrisy of the "Shale Gas Environmental Summit" taking place in London on the 2nd November. The conference event was sponsored by the oil and gas industry and was, according to Frack Off, designed for a single non-environmental purpose, to promote the rapid expansion of fracking.

The action was also planned to coincide with the release of Cuadrilla's report into the earthquakes. "Geomechanical Study of Bowland Shale Synthesis Report" by de Paeter and Bausch, which put together the results of several detailed studies Cuadrilla commissioned in June. The conclusion was that it was highly probable that the company's fracking had caused the two earthquakes.

The same day, 2nd November, activists mounted a separate protest in London. Around fifty anti-fracking demonstrators gathered outside the Copthorne Tara Hotel in Kensington in an attempt to disrupt the Shale Gas Environmental Summit, a grand name for a sales and marketing conference organised by SMI international.

Cuadrilla's response from CEO Mark Miller to the rig occupation was to smear the protestors because they were not local to the area. Which, some commentators thought, was a superb piece of hypocrisy coming from an American.

A further occupation was staged in early December 2011. Eight "cyclists" from Bristol "stormed" the Hesketh Bank site. Three of these, campaigners from Bristol Rising Tide, scaled the rig with supplies and declared their intention to stop the work for several days.

Paul Williams, who works in a Bristol library, was among the protestors. He commented:

"People simply aren't going to stand by and let this crazy extreme sneak into our landscape. We've been inspired by the remarkable work of our neighbours in Wales. Glamorgan county council recently voted unanimously against an application to frack the area. This decision was influenced by Welsh Water's submission that reserve groundwater sites are at risk of contamination. We can stop this before it starts if we act now. If you want earthquakes, runaway climate change, contaminated water, and a threat to agricultural production then fracking's the way forward. If you want energy security and more jobs per kilowatt hour, go with renewables. It's a no brainer."

Sarah, from Bristol, said:

"Fracking is a desperate bid to suck the last, most difficult to reach fossil fuels out of the planet. It is a road to nowhere. The output of fracked wells quickly declines so more and more wells have to be drilled destroying vast swathes of our countryside."

The activists conducted live radio interviews from their perches, and BBC coverage was not unfavourable.

The three came down after thirteen hours and, along with two others, were charged with aggravated trespass.

15 It's all happening in 2012

2012 was a busy year for fracking. For the pro- and anti- frackers, for the government, and for the scientists busy working on two major reports the government wanted to see - an independent review of the Cuadrilla earthquake report, and a new study and report on shale gas by the Royal Society and the Royal Academy of Engineers. The first of these appeared in April, the second in June. It was December, however, before a government decision was taken. The announcement came on the 13th. Ed Davey said fracking could resume. Good news for Cuadrilla.

Not so good for Cuadrilla was the start of the year. On the 11th January in Sussex, their boss Mark Miller came under fire at a public meeting in Balcombe. The Telegraph described it as a "PR car crash". The Guardian said he faced "fury" from the vast majority of the audience.

The Home Counties were now alert to fracking. And they were up in arms. Local residents - estimated between 250 and 300 - packed the Victory Hall. Temperatures rose when the evening started with the screening of a video showing the impacts of fracking in the US.

Miller, flanked by two minders from Cuadrilla's publicity company PPS, faced, according to reports, a barrage of questions, and abuse when his answers failed to please or satisfy the audience. Cuadrilla wasn't the only organisation to come under fire.

Balcombe Parish Council, which had given the nod to Cuadrilla's fracking planning application, was now forming a working party to look into the issues surrounding shale gas. A parish councillor admitted that in 2010 very little was known about fracking. A West Sussex County Councillor said that "procedures had been followed".

Cuadrilla's cohort went away with its tail between its legs.

"This is how they burn witches I guess," Paul Kelly, a director of PPS, Cuadrilla's public relations and lobbying firm was reported as saying, in a PR gaffe that spread across the world as far as Australia. "I can think of dozens of oil companies who wouldn't put themselves through this in a million years and maybe they have it right."

"It has been pretty disastrous," added Nick Grealy, a former wholesale gas salesman who promotes the shale gas industry for clients including Cuadrilla. "They were set up."

One might have more sympathy for Kelly and Grealy's views if they were not complaining about doing a job which as PR mercenaries they were paid to do.

Following the meeting there was a lively debate on the web site gasdrillinginbalcombe.

Anti-fracking resident Kathryn McWhirter drew attention to the dubious way the Parish Council had handled the application, indeed questioned whether it had been considered at all. She asks why Simon Greenwood, who is the owner of the Balcombe Estate which contains the proposed Balcombe fracking site and reportedly earns thousands of pounds per year from Cuadrilla, failed to declare an interest. She says the Parish Council received details of the application on 28th January 2010, prior to the February PC meeting at which the application may or may not have been discussed, but did not reply to a consultation comment request. On 10th March the District Council sent a prompt by email, and received an immediate reply to say yes, fine, go ahead, as Ms McWhirter puts it.

In April 2012 gasdrillinginbalcombe reported that the Parish Council had had a secret meeting with Cuadrilla. This was facilitated by Nick Sutcliffe, a Guildford District councillor and a lobbyist for PPS, Cuadrilla's PR representatives. Private Eye noted that Sutcliffe serves on the planning committee of the Guildford Borough Council and is cabinet member for environmental services. What influence he has in Sussex is less clear.

Gasdrillinginbalcombe served a public information request on Balcombe Parish Council. They suggest their interest is partly because three of the BPC members have vested interests in the fracking industry - Alison Stevenson, who works at Capita Symonds, an organisation which amongst other interests apparently promotes shale gas, Norman Sayer, who works for the fracking industry in Oman, and Mostyn Field who works for WesternGeco, which provides seismic surveying to the fracking industry.

Rodney Saunders, co-chairman of the Council and working group member, oversaw the secret meeting, and appointed three members with vested interest to the working group.

Naturally these accusations caused further stir, with Alison Stevenson coming to the council's defence.

Whatever the rights and wrongs of local infighting - and sleaze theorists have also pointed out that Balcombe's MP Francis Maude, was instrumental in appointing fracking czar Lord Browne to a position of central influence in government - the BPC report was issued in May 2012.

The report is largely intended to provide information on the fracking process. There are a couple of statements of interest. The first, in discussing Cuadrilla's fracking fluid cocktail:

"Both polyacrylamide and biocides contain toxins that are hazardous. In concentrated form these materials require special handling."

The working party clearly wouldn't agree wholeheartedly with Cuadrilla's claim that "What we're putting into the ground is non-hazardous".

And, in dealing with flowback fracking waste, the report says:

"At present Cuadrilla's plans are not sufficiently advanced for it to identify its proposed method of processing the flowback at the Lower Stumble site." - yet another reference to the fact that Cuadrilla can not even in a testing phase tell us how their waste is to be disposed of.

Cuadrilla's claim to be able to complete drilling in six weeks seems at variance with their evidence to the ECCC that their first well had taken 90 days in Lancashire, and the second in the same location was expected to take 45-60 days. This might not seem significant, but it does impact on expected traffic movements.

The working party had this to say on local benefit:

"In general terms, it appears that there will be no direct benefit to Balcombe from oil production at the Lower Stumble site. It would not increase local employment as modern drilling techniques necessitate the use of specialists who are brought in as required. It may be the case, under current planning legislation, that a condition of further planning permission will require certain infrastructure contributions to be made by Cuadrilla or any successor, but they are likely be nominal at best."

The working party report seems fairly impartial in its outcome. Certainly it was not bending over to appear favourable to Cuadrilla's proposals. Nick Grealy praised it, however, perhaps because he was fearing worse.

Possibly because of adverse publicity locally, as well as their moratorium on fracking, Cuadrilla found themselves saying for the rest of the year that they had no current plans for any activity at Balcombe.

In October 2012 Balcombe Parish Council published their results from a survey they had carried out to weigh local opinion. 82% of respondents to the door-to-door polling card delivery expressed the view that the Parish Council should oppose fracking. 95% indicated that they had read the working group's report. The Parish Council vowed to reflect the poll's result in future consultations.

In the Fylde, 2012 gave another taste of Cuadrilla's working methods, and a glimpse into how true their claims to be a good neighbour are.

Cuadrilla carried out a Geophysical Survey over some four months in the first half of the year. The intent of the survey was to find out more about the subsurface geology - the layers of rock beneath the surface.

Cynics might say that they should have done this before starting any drilling and fracking.

The survey required installing various pieces of equipment around the area, including geophones, which we can think of as microphones. When an explosive charge is detonated the reflections from below ground are picked up by the geophones to help give a map of what's down below. A second way of communicating with the geophones is by using vibrating plates underneath vehicles, sending vibrations below ground, again to be reflected and picked up by the geophones.

Residents were not impressed when a host of foreign workers descended on their local area and started laying cables in the roads and accessing fields (sometimes without owner permission) to bore holes for explosive charges. They were not keen on their houses being rocked by explosions, and in some cases damaged. Their children and pets were frightened.

If this seems an exaggeration, I can say two things. Firstly, the local MP Mark Menzies suddenly found himself facing a barrage of complaints. This so concerned him (whether for his constituents' welfare or for the future safety of his seat makes no difference) that he has on more than one occasion subsequently raised local concerns in the House of Commons.

Secondly we can look ourselves at the issues raised by individuals. Here are samples, starting in early April, courtesy of Residents Action on Fylde Fracking (RAFF).

Singleton: *"wires everywhere! French workers tramping over private property putting wires and copper pipes in with GPS attached. No regard for private gardens - no permission sought."*

Anna's Lane 13/4/12: *"Passed by Anna's Lane. Couldn't see down the lane for dust everywhere."*

Singleton 20/4/12: *"Witnessed their work of cabling at Singleton, had to step over a loose cable to enter the newsagent's at Singleton. It had 3 bits of tape when it should have rubber covering that is used on the roads. Started to hit Weeton now and on a public footpath through the fields they used black rather than a visible orange cables. My concern is that if this stage is so shoddy what is going to happen when the real work starts."*

Elswick 23/04/12: *"Tonight we have experienced loud explosions underneath our house which turned out to be caused by the frackers. It was terrifying until we managed to find out, by accident, what was the cause. I have heard that a property has suffered structural damage caused when the frackers appeared next to the house in a field belonging to the house, without permission from the landowner. When they were challenged they simply moved further into the field away from the house. We must stop these people."*

Thistleton, Elswick 28/04/12: *"I am a resident of Thistleton and I am becoming more concerned on what appears to be the secrecy surrounding the whole operation of the testing/ survey works. We have had the orange wires strewn around the fields and across the roads in front of my house for weeks now. We have experienced the loud bangs and tremors that follow with no pre-warning from the company. One morning this week I was woken at 5.20 am to find a van outside with two men checking the rods attached to the cables 5.30 am!! Today my neighbour has had a phone call to say that there will be some larger bangs (explosions) and that they will be monitoring them to see if any damage is caused to property foundations . We have had NO notification, does speaking to one household constitute informing the public or local residents? This whole operation needs to be more open and our local council needs to be more involved in getting this stopped before damage is done."*

Greenhalgh, Kirkham 18/05/12: *"Six explosions yesterday, four this morning, all of which shook my house. No warning from Cuadrilla regarding these. Too much secrecy and misinformation from this company."*

Weeton Road 28/05/12: *"I would like to report that over the weekend (Sunday morning) engineers associated with the gas exploration activities working on behalf of/for Cuadrilla were trespassing on private property/land without prior consent, parking vehicles on privately owned driveways (blocking cars entering and leaving the properties) on Weeton Road. Later on Sunday, testing on Weeton Road was undertaken, which seemingly involved heavy vehicles pounding the road to release pulses in to the ground. This caused all of the four properties at 1-4 Stanley House Barn to shake for 7-12 seconds, 4-5 times, until all residents demanded that the testing was stopped due to fears over the impact that this was having. The shaking to each house was horrendous and felt throughout each property. Having initially approached the first of the onsite engineers, they responded to say that they "didn't speak much English", disregarding the requests of the residents to suspend the work and instead deciding to simply ignore us. No fore-warning or advance notice was given, other than the generic leaflets which greatly mis-represented the actual impact of the testing and consequences. Having finally identified an English-speaking engineer, who provided greater information and whom had seemingly been monitoring the testing from a nearby property (but not at 1-4 Stanley House Barn), calls for the suspension of the testing on Weeton Road were eventually heeded, although it is believed that the testing had actually been fully completed at this point in time anyway. According to the engineer monitoring the output at the nearby property, all of the results were 'within agreed tolerance levels'. Given that what was felt by the residents at the time was well beyond what anyone would consider acceptable, grave concerns have been raised regarding the testing and its impact on our properties, as well as how this is being measured and the overall future activities of Cuadrilla (and accuracy of presented information)."*

Westby 01/06/12: *"I live in Westby and fracking has begun, or I believe it has as recently cables and poles have been posted on our lane. No letters have been sent round but I have begun to feel tremors and loud bangs since they have been placed. This is causing my floor to shake in my property. Who can I contact about this as it is giving me serious cause for concern."*

Westby 05/06/12: *"All today – Queens Jubilee - the house has been shaken by loud bangs and vibrated every 5 to 10 minutes. I and several other residents went to see what it was and it turns out it was seismic blasting being carried out within 100 yds of our property. Farmers had given permissions, presumably for a reward and this appalling noise went on all day. TV was impossible to watch for the fly past. I spoke at length to Mark Oldridge, Permit Administrator, at the lack of respect to both Queen and residents carrying this out today of all days. It seems they work 7 days a week. He did point out that newts and blackpool airport were protected however!!. He suggested I contact Mark Miller at Cuadrilla. I have, and the Lancs County Council and Fylde. It seems no one on either council objected to any of this fracking."*

Wrea Green 08/06/12: *"Well 3 huge wagons and machines have been at the side of my house on the road now . They put a huge plate on the ground which made all the ground shake including my house – again! Felt like an earth tremor. We went out to tell them to stop but they just put their hands up and shook their heads. Then we realised they probably couldn't understand us and they weren't English! An American company using European employment and we are letting this happen?"*

Peel Road 11/06/12: *"We live on Peel Road and this week my horse nearly threw me when a boom came out of nowhere, do you know how long we have to endure this please, as I am scared I may get injured? Is there any info on date and times this might be happening?"*

Wrea Green 11/06/12: *"Hearing (and feeling) underground explosions every five minutes – is getting on my nerves AND potentially damaging buildings (such as our own homes, for example). Were 'we' asked for their permission? I don't think we were."*

Kirkham 11/06/12: *"Just to report that we are feeling some very large Thuds and Vibrations in Kirkham today current amount 21 within the last 45 minutes. The whole house is shaking, radiators rattling and the dog whining."*

Boarding kennels near Peel Corner, Blackpool 12/06/12: *"This morning has been horrendous to say the least!!!! Loud bangs followed by even louder bangs that are scaring the dogs to a frenzy. They are panicking & so are we as we cannot foresee an end to whatever it is they are doing. We have 40 dogs on site here and it is like a war zone. We have had no warning of this why can Fylde Borough Council not do something about it, it's ridiculous!!! I saw the large vehicles coming in to Blackpool last night and it was like something from a futuristic horror movie with the area being overtaken by aliens. It sounds far fetched but these are not just bangs they are sonic booms that rattle dishes, walls, floors , windows and the ground outside that you are walking on. This cannot carry on!! What can I do please ????"*

Boarding kennels near Peel Corner, Blackpool 12/06/12: *"Following a phone call from Mr Josh Owens (Cuadrilla) last night who said all he could do was apologise for the "loud bangs" and scaring the dogs in my Kennels, he assured me we wouldnt hear anymore anything like yesterday!!! This morning I received a phone call from Mr David Ibbison (Cuadrilla) who also once again tried to reassure me we wouldn't hear anything again on the scale of yesterday. Well Mr Owens & Mr Ibbison following yesterday's reports once again loud bangs from 2.00pm today to the time of me typing this e.mail 5.15pm we still have extremely "loud bangs"!! As I said yesterday we have 40 dogs on site here and over half of them have had diarrhoea today and this is due to the upset.*

(Wondering if they would like to help us clean up?) I need more than apologies from you Cuadrilla !!!!"

Lytham 12/06/12: *"We've decided to move away from this area to escape the fracking. Anyone want to buy my house? It's a completely evil disgrace and people simply ridicule you as being a cranky crazy if you try to warn them. I'm off, it's too late to save this area or Southport, they're all sleep walking to hell too."*

Greenhalgh, Kirkham 18/06/12: *"Following damage to my property I wrote to Cuadrilla on May 30th. A few days later a message was left on my answerphone from a Mr Ibbotsen saying that they had received my letter and that he would be in touch with me again soon. Since then nothing. I then telephoned Cuadrilla last week and was then told "These things take time" and that she would pass my message to the engineer dealing with these matters and asking him to update me on the progress with regard to these complaints. That was a week ago still nothing. A neighbour nearby had his cistern cracked and this firm contacted him within two or three days, admitted responsibility and sent him a cheque for a new toilet a couple of days later. All these complaints were as a result of these "vibrating plate machines"*

Wrea Green (19/06/12): *"I have had damage to a piece of outside brickwork with a large crack. I suspect I have further hidden damage and have started proceedings against Cuadrilla who have apologised for not having informed local people of the explosions with the requisite 21 days beforehand."*

Kirkham (20/06/12): *"Very loud bangs in Kirkham today (21/06/12) around 4pm-5.30pm-shook whole house, and even made a dining room chair jump up from floor, scared children and neighbours who were previously oblivious to fracking"*

Near Wrea Green (20/06/12):" I heard the Cuadrilla lorries out after midnight last night."

Newton with Scales (21/06/12): *"Loud bangs and thuds causing house to shake during this morning. Quite disturbing. Happened last week too."*

Peel Corner (06/07/12): *"My mother lives at Peel Corner and has been in the centre of the test explosions. She has now noticed cracks around several of her windows which were not present before the testing. I have contacted a solicitor and Cuadrilla have already been out and quickly offered to "decorate"! Naturally we want a proper repair."*

Cuadrilla say on their web site about their survey that safety was an absolute priority, that they were working to strict Health and Safety standards. If they mean HSE standards, then clearly those standards are inadequate. If they are not (and Cuadrilla did not have a H&S director in place at the time of the survey) what do they mean? They say they used a local company, Spectrum Acoustic Consultants, to establish safe distances of working from houses, by testing the use of explosives. This clearly demonstrates that neither Cuadrilla nor Spectrum had any relevant experience. Cuadrilla say the safe distance was set at a mere 50 metres, which doesn't explain their claims that they established "buffer zones" of 250 metres to reduce the impact. Cuadrilla claim that they had teams closely monitoring the levels of vibration and noise to ensure they were within permissible levels. They introduced into their apologia another company to shoulder blame, CGGVeritas, who according to Cuadrilla were at the forefront of safety systems for the geophysical exploration industry.

This could be dismissed as a mere attempt at damage limitation - in response to the practical experience of Fylde residents - if it were not for the fact that it raises a larger issue.

Cuadrilla and government would both claim UK regulation to be about the strongest in the world. They say this totally scotches the idea that the US experience could ever be repeated here. If Cuadrilla were working to HSE standards the experience of geophysical survey shows safety claims to be a sham, in terms both of Cuadrilla's competence and effectiveness of regulation. What regulations were in place to define safe distances from homes for exploding charges of powerful explosive Pentolite? What hope for people of the Fylde and the environment if Cuadrilla are allowed to progress to industrial scale exploitation of shale gas?

16 Papering over the cracks

After their geophysical survey, and the complaints, Cuadrilla boasted their commitment to communities, claiming, on their website, to having mounted a publicity campaign involving over 30,000 leaflets within the general area, and over 15,000 leaflets to residents inside the survey area as and when local work began. They also claimed to have hand-delivered letters providing at least 24 hours notification of work in specific areas. They spent money on newspaper and radio adverts, and operated a Freephone Information telephone line operated on week days to "provide specific information on the work."

All one can say in view of the complaints raised by residents, with their MP and as voiced above, is that Cuadrilla wasted much of their PR budget. That is the charitable view.

As an example of how Cuadrilla spend money on promotion rather than customer care, we might ask what use is there in boasting an information line operated only on weekdays, during office hours, when the survey operations continued at weekends and outside office hours into the night?

Cuadrilla have relied a lot on their PR company, PPS, which prides itself on providing services in "the tougher areas of communication".

They certainly took on a task when they agreed to do the PR work for Cuadrilla, and by implication fracking.

But what did Cuadrilla take on by employing PPS?

PPS has a less than distinguished history in terms of its moral ethos. It was exposed by a 2007 Channel 4 Dispatches documentary (and Evening Standard reports) as bugging private council meetings, forging letters from residents in support of developers and disguising shills as students to help the building company St George obtain permission for more than 700 homes in Fulham.

In another example of their ethics, PPS advised Countryside Properties on crafting a "community newsletter" when they planned to build 650 homes in Rochdale. The Advertising Standards Association found them in breach of the ASA code in the areas of truthfulness, honesty, and substantiation.

Cuadrilla are currently, together with PPS, subject to a complaint to the ASA for their advertising and promotional activities regarding fracking in the Fylde. The result of this complaint has not yet (as of February 2013) been published.

Despite their no doubt high spending with PPS, Cuadrilla is not winning the PR offensive.

Mark Menzies became MP for the Fylde in May 2010. Since then he has lived in St Annes. His Wikipedia entry lists him as having priorities including UK energy security, changing the planning system to empower local communities and limit inappropriate development, and ensuring a vibrant future for the defence industry within the UK. Menzies' own website lists his political interests as energy, defence and food retailing. No doubt the first interest helped him gain a position as PPS to Charles Hendry, Minister of State for Energy and Climate Change, before he was replaced by John Hayes in September 2012's cabinet reshuffle. Commenting on the November appointments of fresh PPSs, Conservative Home, a website owned by Lord Ashcroft, said this made about 40 locked in by their posts to the "payroll vote", and 21 of these were from the new intake of 2010. This was probably record speed for new MPs to be offered preferment, with the conclusion being that the Whips' Office was nervous about the new intake being independent-minded and wanted to keep them in line.

In other words, a shaky coalition government needed to buy the cooperation and loyalty of new MPs like Menzies.

In September 2011 George Monbiot posted in his Guardian blog an article entitled "The UK's lack of fracking regulation is insane". Monbiot raised many issues about fracking including contamination, water supply and climate change.

Charles Hendry felt obliged to counter this, and comment in the Guardian. Under the rather limp title of "The potential for shale gas is worth exploration", Hendry asserted "The industry is governed by one of the most robust and stringent regulatory frameworks in the world." This deserves some analysis and comment, and we'll come to that later.

Monbiot complained in response that Hendry had failed to address two major issues, firstly climate change and the concern that methane emissions from shale gas could be much greater than conventional gas emissions, and secondly that the world's minerals companies had already found far greater reserves than we can afford to burn without triggering climate breakdown. Monbiot describes his other beefs, for example the Environment Agency refusing to answer some questions regarding chemical test results, and answering others by quoting from Cuadrilla's web site.

Hendry's response to Monbiot was also posted on DECC's web site, where it still remains. He also said in his article:

"We are not taking anything for granted and we remain vigilant to ensure current and future operations remain safe." and *"Any development will not temper the government's firm and unbending commitment to safety and environmental protection and must sit with our plans for a strong portfolio of energy sources as we move to a low carbon economy, including renewables, nuclear and clean coal and gas."*

Fine words, and no doubt when Mark Menzies joined Hendry a couple of months later he was impressed by and shared this view.

Hendry was not blinded by the attractions of shale gas, however. Whatever he has said when he was in office, his attitude changed when he was replaced. In October 2012 he was widely quoted as saying that whilst as a minister he had recognised the ongoing need for gas, the future could not depend on gas. Shale gas could not bring the same benefits as in America and would result in community backlashes. A golden age for gas didn't mean it would come cheap, and "betting the farm" on shale gas would bring serious risk of future price rises.

Back in November 2010 new PPS Menzies wrote a guest column for the Lancashire Evening Post on energy. I think we can see how his mind was working and how his thoughts inclined to Cuadrilla from what he said, repeated on his website:

"A new era of British energy production is upon us and I'm proud to say that Lancashire stands at the very heart of it.

"With an increasing global commitment to reducing carbon emissions and an expected reduction in the use of fossil fuels over the coming decades, new power sources are needed to run our homes, our businesses, our transport; indeed our whole society.

"And Lancashire, with its diverse sources of energy production, can certainly make a huge contribution to that need.

"Vitally to the locally economy too, energy has created and will continue to create, hundreds of jobs across the region."

"In February 2011 Mark Menzies visited Cuadrilla's test site. Menzies admitted concerns had been raised by constituents following a documentary about shale gas drilling in America. His comments following his visit indicate both his wish to be seen as promoting his constituents' interests and his confidence in the system.

"I urged Cuadrilla to carry out more public consultation to let people know exactly what they are doing.

"I was very keen to get the message across to them that they have to be entirely open and clear about the process.

"It is a very strictly controlled activity and the company have had to go through a very meticulous planning process with Lancashire County Council to be allowed to explore the possibility the area could be viable for shale gas.

"They certainly approached the meeting in an extremely professional manner and were keen to show me the measures they have taken at the site at Singleton which ensures the drilling is controlled to the highest possible safety standards.

"Communication is clearly improving significantly and the company have promised me they will be engaging with local people.

"I also welcome the enquiry into this activity by the Energy and Climate Change Select Committee.

"Energy security is an important issue but any new technologies which meet that must be subject to proper scrutiny."

Menzies did take time out in March to recognise action which people could take regarding winter heating bills. A photo opportunity with Sian Lloyd was used to draw attention to the fact that 19% of households in the Fylde, 25% in Wyre and 29% in Blackpool, were missing out on free or cut-price home insulation, a message he repeated in January 2012.

In June 2011 Menzies welcomed the decision by Cuadrilla to voluntarily "postpone" their fracking operations at Preese Hall after the earthquakes, and repeated on his blog a Cuadrilla press release, ending "Cuadrilla remains certain that its operations are completely safe for people, property and the environment."

In March 2012 two of Menzies' interests coincided. In an interesting article he advised farmers to think carefully before submitting planning applications for wind turbines. Why? Because they might face opposition from the Ministry of Defence, who claimed turbines could interfere with vital radar equipment.

In April Menzies reacted to the release of DECC's report on the seismic risk of fracking by saying "Britain needed to set a 'gold standard' for regulation of the industry if it is to proceed."

Presumably he felt the need to say this because he did not at the time believe that such a standard was already in place.

At the end of May 2012 Menzies reported that he had set up a meeting with Residents Action on Fylde Fracking (RAFF) to discuss their concerns over potential shale gas exploitation. He met four of RAFF's committee plus Mike Hill, a local chartered engineer who had been studying shale gas and its challenges to the Fylde. Hill had earlier been technical advisor to Fylde Borough Council on the issue.

Menzies records that this meeting followed a meeting at No 10 with Charles Hendry and PM David Cameron. Menzies had called for a shale gas strategy group to be set up that would oversee all the relevant departments, and this was now in place. It is unclear, in view of later events, what was the nature and composition of this group. What Menzies said is also indicative that he was becoming les than 100% convinced that we currently had full protection under existing regulation, or that the various agencies involved with fracking had adequate coordination.

"Coordinating between DECC, the EA, and the HSE who are responsible for various aspects of regulation, is extremely important, and I welcome the steps they are taking to ensure this process is properly regulated across all the areas of concern that my constituents have raised."

Menzies declared himself a strong supporter of public engagement with shale gas, and urged people to visit the DECC website and contact Cuadrilla directly. This has followed a trend noted earlier by George Monbiot, that DECC and EA were becoming overfond of referring people to Cuadrilla rather than answer questions themselves.

In May 2012 the Blackpool Gazette had taken up the question of residents' complaints with Cuadrilla. Cuadrilla issued a statement which started off, "We apologise to anyone who has been surprised by the brief 'thuds' resulting from our geo-physical survey across Fylde, currently operating around Elswick, Singleton and surrounding areas."

By now we are getting used to Cuadrilla-speak. What to residents were terrifying loud explosions were mere 'brief thuds' to Cuadrilla.

In June Mark Menzies told the Blackpool Gazette that he had called on Cuadrilla to take radical action following complaints by residents. He had found the disturbance unacceptable. Menzies said after speaking to Cuadrilla he was now happy with the measures they would put in place. Of course by now the geophysical survey was nearly over, and Cuadrilla announced on the 27th, less than two weeks later, that they had finished work. It had been running since March, creating three months of problems for residents before Menzies finally stepped in.

Miller said in a press release:

"Following discussions with local people and Mr Menzies I have put in place additional controls to minimise any future disturbance.

"We shall increase the minimum distance between detonations and residences in the built-up areas of Lytham, Wrea Green, Kirkham and

Wesham to 250m, with a distance of 500m used where possible. I've also ordered hours of working for detonations to be restricted to 9am – 6.30pm."

Miller, however, was already out of his top job. On the 15th June the Financial Times reported that he had been removed as CEO and would be replaced by Francis Egan. Miller was demoted to director of the Bowland shale programme. Egan is a head-hunted smooth talker with experience from working at Marathon Oil and BHP Billiton Petroleum. The Telegraph took a sanguine view, giving their readers the option of believing that Francis Egan, Cuadrilla's new CEO, was either an "energy maven shaping the future of Europe's embryonic fracking industry", or an environmental criminal who wouldn't stop drilling until Blackpool blew up.

On appointment, Egan told the FT, "My first priority will be to ensure Cuadrilla continues to listen to and work with our local communities in Lancashire." Plus ça change…

17 Fiddlers and zealots

Whilst residents were fuming about Cuadrilla's activities, the Fylde District Council was working on its own variation of fiddling while Rome burned. They set up a scrutiny committee study on fracking, having finally realised the issue was commanding public interest.

The resulting report, dated April 2012 and adopted the following month, raises in its conclusions some questions for government. While it is easy to be cynical about a relatively low-level council like FBC, and whether a Conservative controlled council was more driven by the need to pacify its population than the belief that it could change government policy, the conclusions read well for the local residents:

"If the shale activities are to go into full production, it is imperative that a strong, robust and comprehensive regulatory framework and best practice arrangements are put in place/ established to deal with onshore activities. The confusion surrounded by the inspection and monitoring arrangements needs to be urgently addressed and the group is of the view that this can only be done by the appointment of an independent "Shale Gas Czar" and that the funding of such an appointment would be via a levy on the operating companies. In addition, suitable robust arrangements need to be put in place for the ongoing monitoring, collection, disposal and transportation of waste material and fracked water (including radioactive waste) which includes an appropriate Radiological Impact Assessment on the likely release of RADON. The Group feels that it is imperative that ongoing research be undertaken by Department of Energy & Climate Change into some of the key areas outlined in the report."

Again, like Balcombe Parish Council, their concern could be seen as too little, too late, not to mention passing the buck.

The report quoted Mike Hill as consultant and advisor. He had been generally supportive of fracking in principle. Hill is an independent chartered engineer and director of Gemini Control and Automation, based in Lytham.

But Hill started questioning whether there was sufficient regulation in force, and this shows in the FBC report. Hill was later to go further, to question the whole regulatory regime. In his opinion, the more he looked at it, the more he saw that it was wholly inadequate to deal with fracking.

His concerns regarding regulation are a damning indictment of the government suggestion - and that of the fracking industry - that in the UK we have robust regulation which will ensure the safety of onshore shale gas exploitation. This question of regulation deserves its own chapter, and we'll come to that later. But I think it is fair to guess at this point that his guidance was influential in leading the FBC's scrutiny committee report conclusions.

On May 17th FBC approved the scrutiny committee report. They had paid lip service to the need to express the concerns of their constituents. At the same time, however, FBC were putting up on their web site propaganda information from Cuadrilla's press releases, and advising residents to contact Cuadrilla or the County Council if they had complaints about Cuadrilla's activities.

It is difficult to tell at the time of writing (February 2013) whether FBC's report had been stuck on a shelf or whether it informed further response by FBC in new developments regarding Cuadrilla planning applications to LCC, on which FBC is a consultee.

A scoping opinion application to a local authority is vital in determining what an applicant has to do in providing an Environmental Impact Assessment in support of their major application. This is a relatively new requirement, and it is no wonder that the public is not aware of what is involved and how they can lodge representations. The same perhaps applies to statutory consultees. In the case of Cuadrilla's Fylde applications one major consultee is Fylde Borough Council, who seem unable to comment, if they are to be judged by lack of response to late 2012 planning applications. Their scrutiny committee report means nothing if it doesn't prompt FBC, rather than the government, to take a stance on fracking and produce a robust response when it matters. They are competent at passing the buck, but not a great deal more, it seems.

As far as the scoping report is concerned, what FBC may or may not have said can be guessed from the response by West Lancs Borough Council to a similar application by Cuadrilla for the Banks drilling site. WLBC said they had no objections. This is extraordinary, and incredibly neglectful, given that Cuadrilla said that their EIA would NOT include -

Socio-economic impacts
Landscape and visual assessment
Noise
Traffic
Archaeology
Climate change
Agricultural considerations.

This is an unbelievable list of exceptions. What is worse is that Cuadrilla said that the opinion provided by Lancashire Council had effectively confirmed the topics which were not required to be covered by the ES.

If this is true it is also a damning indictment of the County Council's planning department.

It could be argued that because this was a scoping report for a variation on an existing permission this could be a different situation from that at Anna's Road (the one within FBC's boundaries). But Cuadrilla's application to reduce the scope of its EIA for Anna's Road, which is effectively a new application, not just one for variation of conditions, is identical in its list of items to be excluded.

In my view FBC was also negligent at the time of Cuadrilla's 2012 geophysical survey in passing any and all complaints on to the LCC or Cuadrilla rather than responding to them. Whilst it might be true that they themselves have no direct authority or responsibility, it beggars belief that if significant planning applications, possibly for large scale industrial exploitation of the Borough are expected in the future, the Council should not take all possible steps to ensure that its officers and councillors were aware of issues raised by their Borough constituents. The impression given is that FBC does not want to know, and nor do its councillors. If this is a wrong view, it is up to FBC to act and show this is the case.

In January 2011 the local Green Party called a public meeting to look at fracking. Only 30 people attended. In mid-2012, a public meeting was called for. MP Mark Menzies took credit for calling it, he chaired it and stacked the "experts" table with representatives of the regulatory authorities, leaving local group RAFF off the top table. The meeting happened on 25th July. This time so many packed the hall - at least 200 - that the room was overflowing and many people were turned away.

Probably the best relatively unbiased account of the meeting appeared on Counterbalance.org.uk. The writer there is well known in the Fylde for his interest in - and sometimes rather scathing views on - local politics. Up until recently he was inclined to support Cuadrilla and fracking unless some data he could get his teeth into changed his mind, and he has been sceptical about climate change.

On this occasion his first observation was the unsatisfactory nature of the way the meeting was planned. There was no opening address by the speakers, and the meeting launched straight away into a question and answer session. Because the government and regulator representatives were not a single voice it was rather untidy. These were Steve Molineaux, Area Environment Manager, Environment Agency, Simon Toole, Director of Licensing, Exploration and Development, Oil and Gas Division, DECC, Steve Walker, Head of Offshore Safety Division, Health and Safety Executive and Stuart Perigo, Group Head of the Development Management Group, Environment Directorate, Lancashire County Council.

This puts the general problem together in a nutshell. With fracking regulated by three organisations, all with different briefs and agendas, and additional responsibility by LCC in giving planning permits, how is it possible to get proper coordination between all of them (a point which has not been lost on Mark Menzies)? And as far as HSE are concerned, Steve Walker's title is just not accidental. The main - one is tempted to say just about the only - experience the HSE have, is in offshore gas, not onshore. This is a serious concern when we come to look at whether not only regulation but also monitoring is adequate.

Lined up against these was Tony Bosworth, a senior campaigner on UK Climate for Friends of the Earth. And Mike Hill, who had advised FBC, whose attitude to-date had been generally in favour of shale gas going ahead *if* it had proper regulation. And of course Mark Miller was there to field questions aimed at Cuadrilla.

Mark Menzies opened the proceedings and according to web commentator 'Counterbalance', said "his own position was that he still had questions about the process and unless he received satisfactory answers to them he would not support it."

The first question from the audience was why were there no local representatives on the panel. The answer was that that was the way Menzies wanted it so that people could receive expert advice.

As his account of the meeting goes on, clearly Counterbalance became frustrated that a lot of people in the audience were against fracking. He comes out with the statement that to him a number of people in the audience were "zealots" with their own agenda and some wanted to use the issue for ends that are entirely unrelated to shale gas.

Time and time again this is an argument used to attack those who are against shale gas. It was used at Balcombe, when the 'anti-brigade' were accused of bussing people in from Brighton.

I can see that it may be true that some of those looking at fracking from the point of view of who holds the power and who makes the decisions take the issue beyond the immediate, and widen the debate on how shale gas is a symptom of our society and government and the way it operates. But that is not the same as saying therefore people with a broad view are wrong, or are "zealots". I think also that the reason Counterbalance would be wrong, Mark Miller was wrong and Francis Egan is wrong (he told the Telegraph that the case against fracking had been "commandeered by extremists") in thinking it is unreasonable for people outside the area to "interfere" in a local issue is this. What happens in the Fylde potentially impacts us all, wherever we live in the UK. In my research I have found many individuals who had no agenda prior to their interest in and research into fracking, who previously held quite liberal views, and could certainly not be described as extremists, then or now.

Country Life is hardly the publication you would expect extremists and zealots to use as a vehicle for complaints. But in September CL published a letter from Fylde resident Mark Mills. It included the following:

"When undertaking the geophysical survey, the employees of the company concerned came onto my land without permission and installed wiring and stakes in some 40 locations. Despite ordering them to desist, they set off explosive charges near my garden, resulting in considerable physical damage…The railroading of our government should be banned…"

Prompted by his experience, and having investigated fracking more, in an open letter Mr Mills expressed the thought that Lancashire and Manchester residents were sleepwalking into disaster.

Mr Mills is still pursuing a legal claim against Cuadrilla. The case is perhaps prejudiced in Mills' favour by the fact that Mark Miller issued a letter of apology for trespass.

Counterbalance summed up his experience of the July public meeting saying that as a positive outcome the meeting had given the opportunity for objectors to let off steam and let regulators and Mark Menzies know the extent of the concerns. But on the negative side he saw opposition hardening because of input from people who were running a different agenda, a rather curious and mistaken view, it seems to me.

RAFF's report on the meeting is interesting to quote. It's hardly the comments of a group of frenzied extremists.

"The people of Fylde have spoken and have told Mark Menzies, Cuadrilla and the bodies who regulate the industry that they are not confident that fracking can be carried out safely in the Fylde. The Question Time-style event, organised by Mark Menzies, was held at the United Reform Church St Annes, on 25 July. And what a turn out! Over 260 people turned up; others couldn't get in and stayed outside trying to listen to the discussions through open windows.

"The panel was: (list)

"Questions were raised about shale gas and the lack of onshore regulations, gas and renewables, the effect the process could have on local residents' health, the environment and housing, and more.

"Were the police expecting trouble? The CCTV crew turned up again – we're getting quite used to seeing them wherever we have a presence. They were at our lovely peaceful and fun Gathering on Lytham Green last week too. Very puzzling. At a time of police cuts wouldn't they be better employed using this equipment for capturing criminal activity? The debate did get quite heated and one chap got carried away and strode down the aisle to make his point, but it was a well behaved and knowledgeable audience that put the panel through their paces. In many cases individuals showed that they were clearly more aware of events than the people representing the regulatory bodies. Clearly not the 'Lancashire Nimby Numpties' one senior person called us at a conference in Durham a few weeks ago!

"Of course RAFF would have preferred a place on the panel – after all over the last few months we have been closer to the people of Fylde on the issues of fracking than anyone. Mark Menzies did direct some questions to us and as mentioned above, the quality of questions from the audience was generally first class.

"Talking to people in the hall before the debate began, it became apparent that the majority of folk in favour of fracking were mainly Conservative councillors. Other individuals were neutral and there to find out more about the process, but the audible intakes of breath that were heard around the hall – particularly when Mike Hill was speaking about the lack of any regulations – suggested that they weren't liking

what they were hearing. Talking to people after the event, there was a sense that many believe that the regulatory bodies are letting us down. Certainly, most people did not leave with a sense of confidence in the safety of fracking.

"We're grateful to Mark Menzies for setting this up and persuading personnel from the various regulatory bodies to attend. Clearly the public has an appetite for this sort of event and we hope to see more planned for the near future."

The senior academic who at the Durham Conference referred to the Lancashire opposition to fracking as "aboriginals" and "nimby numpties" was Professor Richard Selley.

Presumably Counterbalance disapproved of the Frack Off action in June (Counterbalance rather amusingly referred to them as the provisional wing of the anti-fracking movement, which he acknowledged was gaining ground). Frack Off are in fact highly articulated as well as motivated. Their web site contains an impressive number of well-researched articles, news, comment and information.

On the 18th June around twenty members of Frack Off blockaded not a drilling pad but a maintenance site for Cuadrilla's drilling rig in Chesterfield, where it was being stored before moving up to the Fylde.

One of the campaigners who locked himself to the compound gate was Joe Reid, 22. His statement read:

"This prioritising of corporate greed over the interests of people and ecosystems while pretending to care about them, has no better poster child than the Rio+20 Earth Summit that starts on Wednesday.

"Twenty years after world leaders met in Rio de Janeiro and promised to address the environmental and social problems afflicting the planet. they will meet again, to promise, again, to do something about the now even worse problems we face. As with twenty years ago they have no intention of actually doing anything that would put a check on the system of corporate exploitation that is destroying the ecosystems we rely on. This is why ordinary people must take a stand to stop the destruction if anything is ever going to change."

Another campaigner, 27-year-old Elsie Walker, said:

"The scale of development proposed is being completely ignored. Cuadrilla wants to drill 800 wells in Lancashire alone. They are one company going after one type of gas. There are several companies going after several types of unconventional gas in the UK and all potentially on a similar scale to Cuadrilla. If this goes ahead, we will witness the industrialisation of the British countryside and the destruction of the land and water on which we depend. We cannot allow this to happen. We need to face reality and start exploring genuine ways of managing our energy needs in a world where cheap and easy fossil fuels are a thing of the past."

The Guardian again quoted Lord Browne, who had defended fracking, saying it would only affect "tiny bits" of the countryside, and potentially bring 50,000 jobs, with Lancashire as the new industry's '"capital". Two gross distortions in one quote. Around 60% of England is now thought to have fracking potential. And even Cuadrilla's people on the front line claim less than 6,000 jobs could be created. It is not difficult to see why, with statements like this coming from a powerful man, some protestors against fracking are driven to direct action. Mark Miller again in the press attacked not what the protestors were saying, but who they were, and the fact they were not locals.

Even Counterbalance was driven, six months after the St Annes meeting, to concede that Cuadrilla were not as open and transparent as he thought. This was after he had considered how Cuadrilla were trying to avoid including significant environmental issues in their EIA for further drilling.

In his commentary he said that despite having earlier been encouraged by Cuadrilla's willing acceptance for a tight regulatory regime, he was now "shocked and surprised" to discover what was in their EIA Scoping Report application. And went on to say that either Cuadrilla did not know what was required of them, or were trying to circumvent environmental regulations. Counterbalance's conclusion was that Cuadrilla should not be driving the EIA.

This was a praiseworthy admission by Counterbalance that he had been misled by Cuadrilla's earlier press-release propaganda. But what else had he expected them to say? That they opposed stringent regulation?

Counterbalance's earlier comment regarding insurance highlights the fact that a number of Fylde residents were becoming concerned, if not about the pollution effects of shale gas, then about the effect that worries about fracking might have on their insurance and property values.

In June 2012 John Johnson, manager of estate agent Farrell Heyworth in the Lancashire town of Poulton-le-Fylde, near one of the main drilling sites, told the Guardian there were many properties coming on the market because owners said they wanted to get out before prices started dropping.

Richard Sexton, a director of ESURV, the UK's biggest provider of residential valuation services, said levels of public awareness about fracking are still low. He added that as awareness increased, fracking would affect house prices, "blighting properties in the areas perceived to be affected".

Whilst he was not concerned about earthquakes (still the main public perception of the danger from fracking) Mr Sexton asked, in a buyer's market who would want to buy in a fracking area?

In September Justin Allitt, of a leading Fylde estate agents, added his voice to concerns, reporting to a meeting of the Blackpool Business Leadership Group that some purchasers and prospective purchasers were pulling out of buying in the area because of concerns over fracking.

Mark Miller was quick to reply to this, saying that in America, house prices had risen in fracking areas because the industry had created strong economies. What he didn't say was so had crime, offences against women, and other matters previously mentioned.

This debate will continue. But the continuing uncertainty about fracking, and whether it will go ahead at an industrial level, can not help confidence in the property market.

As to whether homeowners will suffer because insurance companies will cease to cover risks from fracking, in my opinion we would have to see a serious accident or a build up of problems such as have occurred in the US before that happens. However it is already clear that farmers will not be covered by their normal insurers for risks in leasing their land to fracking companies, a non-farming activity, and extremely unlikely that the fracking companies would themselves guarantee to cover farmers' liabilities over an indefinite future.

18 Green light

After what had seemed an age, for both the anti-fracking movement and for Cuadrilla, it became clear towards the end of November 2012 that the government was going to give the signal for fracking to go ahead.

This disappointed anti-fracking campaigners, who had been misled by reports in May that the government had decided fracking had a limited future.

At that time the Independent reported that the Prime Minister had convened a Downing Street summit to hear from companies including Shell, Centrica and Schlumberger, which have been working on shale gas projects in America and exploring the potential of supplies in Ukraine and China.

The message that had come through was that Britain was not in a position to exploit huge shale gas resources and what could be extracted was unknown, but in any event unlikely to be a "game changer". Ed Davey, in particular, was said to have been affected by arguments that fracking had the potential to be hugely controversial without securing major benefits in terms of reducing energy costs or lowering carbon emissions.

However on the 2nd December two press releases were issued which could not have illustrated better the failure of the government to address climate change.

Liberal Democrat Energy Secretary Ed Davey admitted that the battle to keep global warming and climate change in check was being lost.

He said attempts to prevent global temperatures from rising more than two degrees Celsius above the pre-industrial level seemed doomed. The Doha climate change conference he was due to attend ended a few days later in what was seen by most commentators as abysmal failure.

But on the same day that Davey was Doha-bound, the Chancellor of the Exchequer George Osborne was about to announce tax breaks for shale gas fracking companies. Coming just days after the refusal to commit to any target for reduction of carbon emissions, this was unsurprising news. And sure enough, a few days later Osborne announced in his Autumn Statement that frackers would get tax breaks and that fracking would shortly get the green light.

It is not clear why Osborne felt it necessary to give financial incentives to the fracking industry. If his intention was to generate income from fracking for the government it does not make sense to give away taxpayers' money to foreign companies when the frackers themselves had told MPs they did not need support.

Back at the beginning of 2011, when the ECCC was taking evidence from advocates of shale gas production and hopeful operators, the committee asked specifically about the need for financial stimulation of the industry. They were told no.

On the 1st March, the question was asked of Andrew Austin, CEO of IGas Energy (a producer of Coal Bed Methane - CBM - the twin sister of shale gas) and Cuadrilla's Dennis Carlton:

*"**Q174 Albert Owen:** A final question to you. You mentioned the finances. Have you had discussions with Government about tax breaks for the industry?*

***Andrew Austin**: We have not had any direct discussions with Government about tax breaks. We do fall within the Small Fields Allowance in terms of the lack of application of supplementary charge, so we are seeking to demonstrate that we can make it economic at the current tax rates and under the current regime. But obviously as the business develops it does have a large contribution to make for UK Plc in terms of jobs, economic activity and security of supply.*

***Dennis Carlton**: Yes, we echo those same sentiments; there is no need at this point in time for incentives to be put in place."*

Nick Grealy is a gas marketing man, a staunch and vocal supporter of fracking, unsurprisingly given that he numbers Cuadrilla amongst his clients. His view on this, too, was quite firm:

Q: *"The US stimulated the shale gas industry with tax breaks from 1980 until 2002—are tax breaks necessary to stimulate the shale gas industry in the UK?"*

A: *"I don't think that tax breaks are necessary, on the contrary as I pointed out, tax revenues would be impacted positively at the national level. The main help government could provide would be to ensure that local planning restrictions take into account the over-riding national interest of energy security. Even there, I believe that existing planning law already has provision for this."*

So no tax breaks were considered necessary. But there was a very nasty sting in the tail, and one which may yet come to pass in 2013. Local planning decisions could be taken away from local councils. We don't need your money, Grealy's message was, but we would like you to undermine local democracy.

Back from Doha, it was left to Davey to announce on the 13th December that shale gas fracking could resume. His script said that shale gas was a promising new potential energy resource for the UK. It might contribute significantly to energy security and substitute for imports which are increasing as North Sea gas is decreasing. He said impacts on water and local air pollution were already covered by the UK's "stringent" rules on oil and gas. Osborne's puppet had spoken. Cuadrilla could start planning more test fracking - and drumming up more financial support for their activities.

In May 2010 the then newly-elected Prime Minister David Cameron said he intended his government to be the "greenest ever". What exactly he meant by that isn't clear, but the announcements at the end of 2012 showed this to be patent nonsense, despite the fact that in April Cameron was trying to tell ministers at a London energy summit that he had achieved his aim. Cameron also said on that occasion that he "passionately believed" renewable energy was vital to the UK's future and would be among our cheapest energy sources in years rather than decades.

People might have been excused for thinking that the decision in favour of supporting fracking was the most appalling hypocrisy, the best example they could find of a PM saying one thing and overseeing policies which did the opposite.

But they'd have been wrong. In 2011 the introduction of the Localism Bill had promised to devolve more power to local councils and communities. It specifically made provision for planning to become more democratic and effective, recognising that current planning rules didn't give people enough say in significant decisions affecting their lives. Yet the day after the announcement of the green light for fracking, 14th December, the Telegraph reported that proposals under the new Growth and Infrastructure Bill could include stripping local councils of their rights to determine shale gas planning applications which the government thought were in the overriding national interest.

Now we were left asking - what could have more impact on people than turning their rural landscape into an industrial zone, having them face unquantified risks of water and air pollution, and all the other risks of fracking?

The Localism Bill was hailed as doing one thing. Action on fracking, centralising decision making did another. With such apparent hypocrisy at the highest level, no wonder many now look at government pledges of ensuring a strong regulatory system as not worth the paper they're printed on.

Certainly earlier there were proposals to widen the scope of the planning regime for nationally significant infrastructure projects (NSIPs) to include large-scale onshore oil and gas extraction projects, and consultation announced on a new streamlined 'one-stop-shop' service and on reducing the number of bodies developers need to consult on every application.

In the House of Lords, Baroness Hanham, a sponsor of the Bill, suggested, in response to a question by Baroness Parminter, that decisions over applications to frack for shale gas will not be added to the fast-track regime for major infrastructure. Yet.

Speaking on the 4th February 2013 in the House of Lords during the Growth and Infrastructure Bill's committee stage, Hanham said: *"At present, fracking decisions will not be taken out of the hands of local authorities. Any developer will have to consult the local community and local people and the local authority will have the right of determination.*

"A request would have to be made to the secretary of state to use the infrastructure regime and he would agree to such a request only where the proposal raised issues of national significance.

"It may be that national significance and fracking will be one and the same but that gives an indication that at present we would expect this to be dealt with locally and local people would have a big say in what was to happen."

Few opponents of fracking or believers in the importance of local democracy will see this statement as giving them any encouragement.

Back in the previous October, Mark Menzies had secured an adjournment debate on fracking in parliament. An adjournment debate is a fairly pointless exercise, but it gives an opportunity for MPs to show their constituents that they are batting for them.

After the customary anodyne opening remarks, Menzies made it clear that he did not regard current UK regulation and procedures as adequate. He said:

"We still have some way to go before we have a regulatory system in place for any potential stage of development. We need a system that addresses all concerns, that can be properly enforced and that sets an example to industry across the world. That is particularly important for the UK, where population density will always be a factor."

He went on to say:

"Many of the people who have been involved in the process are experts in their field, but despite that, I do not believe that the regulatory system is robust or transparent enough to instil public confidence should permission be granted to the industry. That is why I am calling for an independent panel of experts to be set up without delay. Many questions and concerns still surround the shale gas process, and it is vital that we have a panel for three purposes: to look at each issue in detail; to fully

appraise the risk; and to ensure that specific regulations are in place to deal with that. If part of the process cannot be dealt with safely through regulation, an alternative method should be found. If, however, an alternative way of carrying out that process is not possible, it must not be done."

Menzies made another request - that Environmental Impact Assessments be made compulsory, regardless of size, and asked whether similar health impact assessments were under consideration. He stated clearly that in his opinion the Anna's Road site was totally unsuitable for production, and expressed concern about the industrialisation of the Fylde. He had made a good attempt to represent the Fylde's concerns.

Minister John Hayes brushed off a number of concerns about fracking, and returned to the central plank of the pro-fracking argument as it now stood - the idea that the report into seismic activity and the "Royals" report both said that fracking could continue with best practice and firm regulation. He insisted that there was already a strong regulatory framework in place, and a stringent planning process. He confirmed there was a strategy group to ensure coordination of the existing regulators. During this speech he introduced the story that Wytch Farm was the biggest onshore oilfield in Europe. At the same time he encouraged the idea, without being explicit, that shale gas would bring UK consumer energy costs down.

In short, Mark Menzies had made his stand on his constituents' behalf, and got the answer that was expected.

Along with the Autumn Statement was an announcement that an Office for Unconventional Gas would be set up. Menzies claimed this as a victory for his calls for such a single body to take responsibility for shale gas. But there were two snags. Firstly it was not an independent body, as Menzies had requested, and secondly it was set up with a clear brief to provide a one-stop-shop to facilitate investment in shale gas. It was intended to prioritise drawing in more shale gas money, not to oversee and tighten regulation and coordination of the various bodies involved - DECC, DEFRA, EA and HSE. Menzies had in fact lost his cause.

That is, of course, not how it was put by Ed Davey, who on the 13th December side-stepped a question in Parliament by Menzies about the independence of the new body and whether it would impose new regulation. He said only "One of its jobs will be bringing together the various regulatory bodies so that they are properly co-ordinated, and our work as we approach potential commercial development in a few years' time will include ensuring that we have all the regulatory controls that we need."

A minute earlier Davey had said "It is very important for us to take the public with us as we explore the potential for shale gas in the United Kingdom."

The writing was on the wall. The government was determined to pursue shale gas. There was no "exploration of potential" in the government's mind. All it wanted was to find a way of overcoming public opposition.

It wasn't going to be that simple.

19 Court and protest - UK style

There was one shred of comfort for the anti-fracking movement. The Telegraph headed its report on the green light for fracking with:

"Cuadrilla rapped for management failings as Davey gives green light to shale gas exploration."

Energy Secretary Ed Davey had told Cuadrilla to address management failings before it continued fracking in Lancashire.

Investigations had found problems with communications between Cuadrilla managers and its board, on which former BP chief Lord Browne sits. DECC said these related to the "possible cause of the earthquakes and options for mitigation" and added, "This lapse had not, in this case, caused a serious safety or environmental problem but if left unaddressed the underlying causes would compromise Cuadrilla's future ability as an operator."

It was acknowledged that Cuadrilla had since made changes, including the replacement of Mark Miller by Francis Egan and the appointment of a board member for Health and Safety. But Davey said there was a review in progress by external consultants, and Cuadrilla would not be granted final consent for fracking until that was complete.

The release of correspondence between Charles Hendry and Lord Browne under the Freedom of Information act makes it clear how seriously the minister at least had taken the matter:

"Dear John

"You will be aware that my Department is concerned that Cuadrilla failed to recognise the significance of the casing deformation experienced in the earth tremor triggered by fracking operations on 1st April 2011. So much so, that the company did not report it my officials in contemporary discussions as to the possible cause of the tremor and the possibility that it might be linked to fracking. In the light of Cuadrilla's responses to the Department's subsequent enquiries, I have formed the view that this

failure discloses weaknesses in Cuadrilla's performance as a licensee, which need to be addressed.

"I would like to discuss these matters with you, your Chief Executive Officer, and the Board representative of AJ Lucas, as soon as may be convenient, to hear what improvements you might propose to address these concerns, and how these might best be implemented.

"Perhaps your office could contact my diary manager to arrange a suitable date.

"(Handwritten) I very much hope we can resolve this in the near future."

Browne's reply, two weeks later on the 25th May 2012, contains the information that Cuadrilla has constituted a new H&S committee, replaced its CEO and created a number of new senior roles such as the Director of Communications. Critics may be forgiven for wondering what a boss of BP was thinking of when he let his team loose on the Fylde without setting up an appropriate company structure. Frack the Fylde first, worry about the fallout later?

Browne goes on to say that Cuadrilla had established and communicated a clear policy that operational incidents "judged to have a potentially serious impact on health and safety or infrastructure integrity" would be reported to DECC immediately. Which rather begs the question of how serious an "incident" has to be before it is reported.

Browne, who had headed a multi-billion company (but had not accepted the blame for what has been described by some as implementing cost-cutting safety reduction which contributed to major BP disasters), was not able or willing to set up a small company which saw integrity as its top priority, when they knew they would be at the spearhead of fracking in this country. To my mind this displays just as much bad judgement from Browne as when he insisted on lying to the High Court about his personal affairs. He should have taken the fall for Cuadrilla's cover-up, rather than Mark Miller. But that is obviously not the way it works in the world of the powerful.

Ed Davey might also have asked the experts whom he invited later to look into Cuadrilla to consider what emerged in Preston Magistrates court in September 2012.

Three protestors were on trial for an occupation on 1st December 2011 of Cuadrilla's Banks rig.

This wasn't the first trial of protestors - the 2nd November occupation had resulted in charges of aggravated trespass against three of the protestors who were bailed out of Lancashire. Curiously another two, who were Lancashire residents, faced no charges. In July the three protestors mounted a defence of "necessity" but were convicted.

However, with the trial of the December Hesketh Bank protestors events took a new turn. The defence was mounted to show Cuadrilla had acted unlawfully. The charges were aggravated trespass, and the prosecution was required to show Cuadrilla were acting lawfully for charges to stick.

In court to give evidence, a senior planning officer confirmed that Cuadrilla had continued its operations outside the period of their planning permission. He also confirmed that they had breached a condition of the permission relating to safeguard bird life in the adjacent Ribble Estuary protected site.

According to court reports, DECC, the licensing authority, gave evidence that it uses the offshore oil regulations to licence onshore fracking operations and stated that they are not interested in policing breaches of environmental law, which is the job of the local planning authority and the Environment Agency. The local council planning officer made it clear in his evidence that he only had limited resources and few powers to police developers. The general expectation from the regulators is that companies will regulate themselves.

This raises the questions - why did Lancashire County Council allow Cuadrilla to drill two months after the expiry of the permitted period? Did they even know this was happening?

This is just one example of how in the UK regulations are in practice totally inadequate, in particular in terms of coordination between the various agencies, and lack of resources to monitor breaches. In addition, regulation (and HSE operation and funding) is geared up to offshore oil and gas practices, not onshore.

In Preston court, the issue was ducked. Two of the activists were released for the reason that charges against them had been poorly framed. It is surprising that it took nine months for this to be discovered, but it saved the court from passing judgement on the legality of Cuadrilla's operations. The circumstances were interesting. Cuadrilla's "expert" declined to give evidence in their favour.

The prosecution said it had hoped to call Pat Waring, an ecologist employed by Cuadrilla Resources, to attempt to demonstrate that Cuadrilla had not been operating unlawfully at the time of the protest. In the event Mr Waring was not prepared to appear for the prosecution. This left the prosecution with the challenge of trying to demonstrate 'lawfulness' without an expert witness. This was left undetermined as the prosecution failed on the first point of proving the offence with which the protestors were charged, aggravated trespass. They failed to show that there was disruptive action beyond simple trespass.

The third protestor had faced a different charge, of failing to leave land as soon as practicable when asked to do so by a police officer. Zoë Smith was found guilty and fined a total of 1,000 pounds.

She said on conviction:

"This verdict confirms my view that the regulatory authorities are hopelessly inadequate at their job and don't have the protection of the environment as a priority. Companies like Cuadrilla are allowed to flout their obligations with impunity, while concerned citizens are criminalised."

Whatever you may think of that view, it is clear that in Preston one more black mark had been chalked up against Cuadrilla.

Despite the possibility of arrest and court appearances, anti-fracking protestors continued to take direct action. In October 2012 activists scaled two 300 foot tall chimneys at Britain's newest gas-fired power station in Nottinghamshire. On the day of the invasion, around five protestors were arrested and charged with aggravated trespass. But more were successful in scaling the chimneys and setting up camp. They were arrested and charged when they came down three days later. The climate change campaign group "No Dash For Gas" claimed responsibility for the protest.

In November 2012 protestors staged a "die in" outside a fracking conference venue in London. In the same month student protestors mooned a pro-industry speaker when he claimed methane contamination of water in the US was not because of fracking but was because of faults in the pipes bringing the gas to the surface (!).

On December 1st around 300 protestors mounted a demonstration in Westminster, erecting a mock drilling tower in Parliament Square. They also marched to No 10 Downing Street and delivered a letter.

BBC reporter Ben Ando said at the start of his coverage of the peaceful demonstration, "The point they're making is a serious one" and continued to give a fair account of the protestors' position.

He also mentioned a Blackpool man whose house had been damaged by fracking and had come down to London to take part in the demonstration.

This was a reference to Gayzer Tarjanyi, or Gayzer Frackman, as he now called himself, a 51 year old St Annes resident who had cycled down to join the London protest. This wasn't his first trip to the capital for the cause, as we saw earlier. In October he walked all the way from Blackpool to deliver a letter to No 10 Downing Street.

Frackman was not impressed by the response from the PM. After his long walk and heartfelt letter of objection to fracking, this is what he received.

"Dear Mr Frackman

"I am writing on behalf of the Prime Minister to thank you for your recent letter.

"Mr Cameron is most grateful for the time and trouble you have taken to get in touch.

"I have been asked to forward your letter to the Department of Energy and Climate Change, so they too are aware of your views.

"Thank you, once again, for writing."

(signed Correspondence Officer, Direct Communication Unit).

This was Frackman's original letter:

"Dear Mr Cameron,

"Fracking in the Fylde.

"I have walked from Blackpool Tower visiting campaign groups and well sites starting in Lancashire through Wales and on to Sussex before coming to 10 Downing Street to deliver this open letter asking you 10 key fracking questions.

"The manmade earthquake on 1st April 2011 damaged my home in Lytham St Annes, ten miles from the frack site. Given that Cuadrilla admitted its guilt and given the suspension of the test fracking, I am finding it hard to understand now why the "greenest government" seems to be about to allow fracking to go ahead.

"To date I have had no apology from Cuadrilla, despite having been to many presentations and meetings, and despite the fact that Cuadrilla is well aware of my address and of the damage it caused to my property. The government seems to be ignoring the dangers of the fracking process, for us and for future generations, and I wonder if the government's confidence in the fracking industry is misplaced.

"1. Fracking is chaotic and unpredictable. In the only attempt so far at high volume hydraulic fracturing in the UK, almost everything that could go wrong did go wrong. Disregarding the internationally agreed 'Precautionary Principle', the fracking industry is proceeding on a 'suck it and see' basis. Prime Minister, will you make these companies immediately observe and abide by the Precautionary Principle?

"2. Fracking in the Fylde will significantly alter the character and appearance of the area and deny its citizens their right to enjoy their home area at leisure and liberty.

The parliamentary constituency of Witney lies in an area with fracking shale gas potential. Prime Minister, as the constituency MP for Witney, what steps will you take to make sure people's quality of life is not spoiled by industrialising the area with fracking shale gas wells, condensate tanks, waste fluid pits, pipelines, compressor stations, and intense, frequent and heavy road tanker traffic?

"3. When fracking for shale gas in the Fylde damages businesses, communities, homes, health and the environment it is not clear where to go for redress. If damage or loss occurs, the injured parties are left to fend for themselves against a powerful and unresponsive industry. Prime Minister, will you put in place adequate arrangements so that the industry discharges its liabilities promptly and fairly without placing injured parties under unreasonable strain and expense, and will you ensure the establishment of a liability levy that is rigorously regulated and autonomous but industry financed?

"4. There has been no Environmental Impact Assessment of the proposed fracking shale gas wells in the Fylde. The agencies responsible have not explained the reason for this. Without an informed public consent this industry cannot proceed. Prime Minister will you tell the industry and relevant government agencies to come clean about fracking, disclose all relevant information and conduct all appropriate assessments, starting with a full Environmental Impact Assessment covering the whole process of fracking at each site?

"5. Fracking in the Fylde will lead to induced subsidence and damage to homes and property. As is its custom the industry responds to this issue in vague terms. However in the US, because of the risk of fracking subsidence, the federal body responsible for flood control bans any fracking near infrastructure such as dams and embankments. Given the lack of clear information on the subsidence risks in the Fylde, Prime Minister, in the absence of robust freely shared information about subsidence from fracking, will you accept that exploration should be halted?

"6. The industry is secretive or silent about how spent frack fluid is transported, treated, evaporated, injected in to wells and disposed of. Four million litres of radioactive waste water from Cuadrilla's Preese Hall Farm site was moved without a permit, diluted and dumped in the Manchester Ship Canal. Some waste frack fluid has been moved more recently but the public cannot get information about who moved it or where it was moved to and by what permitting process, if any. For proposed future operations it seems Cuadrilla may be planning to store its waste on the frack well site and reinject the waste when the well has

depleted. Prime Minister will you make the industry come clean and disclose fully what arrangements are planned and being made for the storage, transport, treatment and disposal of the fracking industry's biggest problem and expensive headache, toxic and radioactive used frack fluid and produced water?

"7. Hydraulic fracturing (fracking) means building up huge hydraulic pressure to split or fracture shale rock. When the rock splits and the pressure finally is released, a large plume of methane and other hydrocarbons plus cancer causing benzene and other volatile organic compounds (VOC) escapes in to the air. Although new and stringent regulations exist in the US, there are no similar regulations in the UK. Prime Minister will you rectify this and introduce statutory regulations to stop such routine air pollution?

"8. Authoritative US data shows that 30% of well casings fail within 10 years. Failed well casings are a route for contamination to groundwater aquifers and to the air. Fracking shale gas wells are closely spaced with each well covering about 50 acres. Fracking shale gas wells means very high numbers of wells. Prime Minister what rate of well casing failure would be an acceptable rate?

"9. Without pre-fracking baseline testing of air and water, claims for damage caused by oil and gas exploration and production often have failed in the US. Prime Minister will you undertake to introduce statutory independent commissioning of baseline testing before each planning permission is granted for fracking, funded by an industry levy?

"10. In the Fylde 800 plus fracking shale gas wells are planned by Cuadrilla. Because production from fracked shale gas wells declines steeply, 20% more wells need to be drilled and fracked annually just to replace the depleting wells. Prime Minister do you acknowledge that a short-lived supply of fracked shale gas will industrialise and contaminate large areas of the countryside forever?

"Like fracking for shale gas, the extraction of unconventional coal bed methane presents another growing threat to our small, crowded and yet beautiful island. Prime Minister please examine closely the implications of the coal bed methane wells already approved near our friends at Airth in Scotland.

"I've walked more than two hundred miles to bring fracking to your attention. Can the country and especially the countryside count on you to go the extra mile?"

20 The rash spreads

Following the government announcement that fracking could go ahead, the sleeping would-be frackers woke up and started making plans for shale gas testing in areas other than Lancashire and Sussex.

Kent campaigners were alert, and voiced their concern immediately and loudly in the media.

A year earlier, the County Council approved an application by Coastal Oil and Gas Ltd to drill an exploratory borehole for coal methane and shale gas at Woodnesborough, near Sandwich. It was originally stated to be a simple test of coal and shale. Activists warned that it could be the first step towards the use of fracking. At the time some thirty letters of objection had been received from the public, but Dover District Council, Woodnesborough Parish Council, Sandwich Town Council, the Environment Agency and Southern Water had no objections to the plans.

Coastal's director Gerwyn Williams told the BBC that fracking would have to be proven absolutely safe before they would even think about it.

The other threat in Kent is Cuadrilla at Cowden. Although Cuadrilla say they have no plans at present, they did not rule out further exploration at a future date.

Whilst we might take these statements with a pinch of salt, it is significant that the industry now knows fracking is a dirty word.

Other campaigners in the South-East, in Sussex, declared themselves ready for action again as fracking resumption was announced. Their area has the most potential for shale gas outside Lancashire. Cuadrilla maintained, however, they had no immediate plans for Balcombe, although signs were that would change by 2014. The Telegraph reported campaigners and residents of Balcombe were angered by the government decision.

The Sussex Argos said that Sussex was now on the front line of the controversial fracking revolution, and confirmed their "discovery" that 15 licences had already been issued by DECC for exploring the county's reserves. These spanned hundreds of thousands of acres of countryside. The Argos listed the towns of Balcombe, Midhurst, Petworth, Bolney, Haywards Heath, Crawley, Billinghurst, Barnham, Bognor, Uckfield and Crowborough as all being within potential exploration areas.

However the biggest immediate impact of the government announcement on fracking resumption, perhaps - apart from in Lancashire - was on plans for fracking in Somerset.

DECC had granted PEDL licences for exploration in four parts of Somerset and the Mendips covering the towns of Radstock, Shepton Mallet, Wells, Evercreech, Pilton, Midsomer Norton, Wookey, Harptree, Chewton Mendip, Whitchurch, Saltford, Chew Magna, Pensford and Keynsham. In addition Bristol, Glastonbury and Street were potentially affected, sharing the same water supply.

In mid 2011 UK Methane Ltd announced a plan to explore for shale gas in the Mendips. UK Methane shares a parent company, UK Onshore Gas, with Coastal. And the same spokesman, director Gerwyn Williams, who seemed more confident than later in the year. His comments at the time were widely reported.

"I know there's been a lot of controversy over fracking shales, but if you go by the government select committee's report, and the Environment Agency comments, then it is quite safe."

Despite the fact that UK Methane had, together with its partner Australian company Eden Energy, only done some deskwork, they were confident they would create thousands of jobs.

I think we have heard the same story before.

UK Methane's plan didn't go down very well with Bath and North-East Somerset Council, who expressed concern (even though the prospective site for exploration would have been in the Mendip District Council's area), especially over the possible contamination of Bath's world-famous springs. Council leader

Paul Crossley wrote to local MPs and government ministers, the leader of Mendip District Council and English Heritage, warning of potential damage to the springs.

In the event UK Methane concentrated its efforts on a Coal Bed Methane application instead, at Hicks Gate, Keynsham, between Bristol and Bath. The application was to "Drill and test the permeability of the coal and associated strata", and was lodged in late September 2012 with Bath and North East Somerset Council. One can only imagine that the combination of the prospect of local opposition, plus the halt in shale gas exploration, had persuaded UK Methane that they had a better chance of getting a CBM application in under the fracking opposition's radar. That didn't happen. Over 700 people objected to UK Methane's application. So too did Keynsham Town and Compton Dando Parish Councils.

A week after the government gave the green light for shale fracking, UK Methane withdrew its controversial CBM proposal. The bad news was that they promised to return with an application in the new year for production - not just testing - which would include shale gas. UK Methane explained that since the amount of information they had been asked to produce for the exploration drilling was far higher than any other they had been involved with, they felt that for a minimum extra amount of work they should apply for a production licence. January 2013 ended without sign of an application for production being submitted. They are said to be pursuing an ultimate ambition of some 2,000 wells in Somerset, according to a report from Frack Off. I suspect UK Methane will face stiffer opposition than Cuadrilla has met so far in Lancashire. In Somerset there is an active movement coalition against fracking with over twenty local groups opposed to fracking either by direct or indirect support of Frack Free Somerset's efforts. FFS promotes public awareness and conducts workshops, and is currently holding a number of events under the banner of "Frack Free February". It plans to distribute 50,000 leaflets to inform and mobilise opinion in the area. Already a new group is setting up in Chew Magna as a result of the FF February initiative.

At the end of February 2013 UK Methane announced they had postponed their plans for a Keynsham application, to concentrate on work in South Wales. They denied the delay - for at least a year, had anything to do with the force of local opposition in Somerset.

The Keynsham proposal wasn't the first CBM application to have foundered in 2012. Public outrage stopped plans in South Lanarkshire. In March, Reach CSG withdrew their application for drilling on the Devro food processing factory site in Moodiesburn, following hundreds of letters of objection. Residents had feared the application was a stepping-stone to a horizontal drilling under their homes. An article in the Airdrie and Coatbridge Advertiser suggests that a major reason was the landowner Devro withdrawing from their arrangement with Reach.

This did not stop Dart Energy from lodging an application mid-2012 for full CBM production in Scotland, which would be the first full unconventional gas development.

There are also CBM test drilling applications pending at Llantrisant in Wales, and at Eaton, near Retford, Nottinghamshire.

21 Extreme energy - CBM and other unconventionals

The terms "extreme energy" and "unconventional gas" cover a range of new technologies and engineering solutions to the fact that fossil fuels are becoming increasingly difficult to extract - at least at an economic rate that satisfies the fossil fuel industry.

In the term "unconventional gas", the word "unconventional", as the fracking industry often repeats, does not refer to the nature of the gas itself but the source of the gas. As conventional sources of gas have become depleted, the industry has found new sources. Main amongst these are shales, which is what we have been primarily discussing, and also coal beds. A third source, but far less important currently, is so-called "tight gas" where gas is trapped in pockets in low-permeability rocks but difficult to get at.

Extreme energy is a term used to describe energy extraction methods that are newly developed, including Shale Gas, Coal Bed Methane and Underground Coalbed Gasification. New techniques also include Tar Sands, Mountain Top Removal and Deep Water Drilling.

Just as the advocates of shale gas were trying to persuade us that it was good for the environment and climate change, here comes the next energy Big Thing, taking us back to oil dependence. Touted as the next big new technique to revolutionise our energy supplies shale oil "could add £50bn to UK economy" as the Telegraph's hysterical headline put it in uncritical response to a report released on 14th February 2013 by PWC, an aggressive pro-client powerhouse, as they describe themselves.

The process of extracting shale oil offers another environmental nightmare, with serious issues of land use (even more than shale gas because it involves a mining operation to extract the oil shale), waste management and water and air pollution. With techniques like strip mining (similar to open cast) used in accessing oil shale, it would be hard to imagine a new energy technique less appropriate to the UK. Unless it were Underground Coal Gasification, UCG, which involves setting light to coal underground and collecting the produced gases. This possibility is currently being explored and promoted by the government, and various licences have been issued around the coasts of England, Wales and Scotland. (Which raises the question why shale gas, a better-proven technique, should not equally well be considered offshore.) Perhaps in order to minimise opposition, the blocks which have been given UCG exploration licences are just off the coast, close enough for horizontal wells to be drilled from the shore.

However, of the various extreme techniques, apart from shale gas, production of Coal Bed Methane CBM and UCG are the immediate threats to onshore Britain.

Where coal deposits have been worked, but are no longer economic to mine, or where coal seams were too deep, too shallow or too thin to mine, new techniques involving horizontal drilling can make extraction of methane from these deposits possible.

Gas extraction from coal seams has been going on for some time, but previously the gas was extractible by sealing the coal seam and allowing gas to build up in pockets which could then be easily drained. This has helped CBM and more extreme techniques fly in under the environmentalists' radar.

The techniques used can vary depending on the nature of the coal seam. Hydraulic fracturing is one technique which can make a coal seam release its gas. Another method is an injection technique called cavitation. Yet another is - instead of pumping fluids *into* the coal - pumping water *out of* the coal seam, which can be enough to get gas flowing.

The coal seams are generally far closer to the surface than shale gas formations. This raises environmental issues potentially more serious even than shale gas. As Frack Off says:

"The closer proximity to the surface combined with the fact that it almost always involves pumping large quantities of water out of the coal seam (water that has been marinading in coal for thousands of years)

means that the problems with water pollution and leaking methane tend to occur regardless of whether fracking is performed.

"Being closer to the surface the chances of methane migrating to surface (with the effects of fracking) are higher and the large amounts of water that need to be pumped out of the coal seam (produced water) and disposed of somehow, means the chances water contamination.

"The produced water can by up to five times as salty as seawater and contain a wide variety of toxic contaminants. The cost to treat and dispose of the produced water can be a critical factor in the viability of a coal bed methane project (producing a strong economic incentive to cut corners and dump produced water illegally). Also, due to generally being much closer to the surface and the large amounts of water that need to be pumped out of the coal seams, subsidence can also be an issue. The massive pumping of ground water can also negatively affect water tables and aquifer levels."

As with shale gas fracking, CBM has had a history in the US of environmental and social issues.

In the UK, prime targets for CBM production are historical coal mining areas, the North, the Midlands, South Wales and Scotland. But because other areas may have deep coal seams that were not able to be mined previously, additional regions are at risk, including Somerset.

There are more companies interested in CBM who have interests in PEDLs than there are who saw the 13th licensing round opportunities for shale gas - principally Cuadrilla.

These include Dart Energy, IGas Energy and UK Methane.

Andrew Austin of IGas told the ECCC that the company had a pilot scheme producing electricity at Doe Green in Warrington, and had drilled another nine test wells. He claimed that fracking at Doe Green had not pumped in anything other than water. But he said the "water" pumped in was partly recovered from the well. One wonders why the committee did not ask him to amend his statement, particularly as he went on to say that as a natural part of producing CBM you do produce water, which is mildly saline, brackish water. IGas is also expected to enter the shale gas stakes after reporting promising results from its Ince Marshes test drilling near Elton, Cheshire.

Greenpark Energy (bought by Dart) is fracking wells at Canonbie in Dumfries and Galloway.

A valid point has been made that whilst so much attention has been paid to the problems of shale gas, this has taken attention away from the potentially more damaging impact of CBM, with or without fracking. I also plead guilty to the charge that in this book I have focussed on shale gas fracking. CBM is indeed the equally unacceptable twin of shale in the rush for the exploitation of the UK by energy companies who see no further than their profit potential.

A UK parliament briefing suggests CBM large scale production is unlikely before 2016. Shale gas will come later. If the go-ahead is given by local planning authorities to CBM, then CBM will have succeeded whilst shale gas fracking commands the public attention and provides a smoke-screen for an equally undesirable extreme energy practice to start destroying the environment, particularly outside England and outside the Tory homeland of the South of England.

Underground Coal Gasification is, however, already a worry, particularly in South Wales.

The idea of UCG has been around since the middle of the 19th century, but attempts to employ it met until recently with mixed results. However, there is one example of a commercial UCG plant in Uzbekistan which has been producing the synthesised gas since 1961. Photographs of the plant suggest the huge type of industrial facility which would not be acceptable in the UK.

Post WW2 European pilot schemes were largely withdrawn as the energy prices fell. Linc Energy (who run the Uzbekistan plant) constructed and commissioned a demonstration facility in Australia, the largest in the world, they claimed. The site is indeed huge. A test project with CCS is planned for Germany, and a number of others have been carried out in the US.

The basic UCG process consists of drilling two wells into a coal seam. The first is used to inject air or oxygen, so that when the coal seam is set alight in a (hopefully) controlled reaction it is kept burning. The second well collects resulting gases, a mixture of hydrogen, carbon dioxide, carbon monoxide, methane and other gases. These gases are then burned to produce energy.

The heat generated by the combustion process is generally not recoverable, and the carbon dioxide produced is a waste product. The energy produced in the process is less than that obtained had the coal been directly mined, but supporters of UCG claim UCG is environmentally less damaging than coal mining.

Whilst this may be true, UCG is not without significant environmental risks - possible water and air contamination, subsidence, and still a global warming impact.

Coal combustion wastes remain underground and can percolate into groundwater, and this has provided documented examples of pollution which make groundwater contamination one of the main objections to UCG. The risk is there, as with shale gas fracking, whether the evidence comes to light now, or decades into the future.

CCS technology could possibly reduce fears about UCG's greenhouse gas footprint, but this - as with modern UCG itself - remains in its infancy.

A recent technological development has been to eliminate the need for two separate boreholes, one each end of the burn. A single well can be drilled and used both to inject air or oxygen into the horizontal section to fuel the burn, and to retrieve and extract the gases. This would enable offshore coal reserves to be exploited more easily, and this is what the UK has been banking on in granting "offshore" licences.

Fears remain of an untested offshore or near shore activity, and the industrialisation of the coastline. If the government's attitude is that any pollution problems that arise are likely to be confined to our offshore waters rather than to our land as would be the case with an onshore facility, they are careless as to the importance of the marine environment. They also misunderstand or ignore the potential environmental disturbance onshore due to industrialisation of areas by processing plants, pipelines or power generation stations, electricity cabling, traffic, and, above all, the fact that UCG is still a fossil fuel energy process with a significant climate change penalty.

22 Shale gas in Northern Ireland

Most of this book has concentrated on England, for the reasons that this is where shale gas is happening right now, and secondly because the regulation system and laws that we have been looking at are often, but not always, England-specific. It's time to remedy that with an overview of the general UK situation.

Regarding regulation, Northern Ireland is in an even worse position than England.

In September 2011 Friends of the Earth drew attention to the fact that Northern Ireland is currently the only part of Britain or Ireland without an independent regulator and enforcer of environmental legislation, and that a recent consultation exercise carried out by the DOE there revealed that 83% of respondents supported the creation of an Environmental Protection Agency.

FoE director, James Orr, said:

"How on earth are we going to regulate gas fracking when we can't even regulate someone dumping illegally or causing water pollution? The price to pay for a bad record of environmental regulation is that we are simply not capable, without an Environmental Protection Agency, of regulating this type of activity."

FoE noted that:

"A number of petroleum licenses were issued in Northern Ireland in 2011, one of which was for shale gas extraction in County Fermanagh issued to Tamboran Resources Ltd. It is believed that exploration drilling cannot be carried out without additional consents from several regulatory authorities including DETI, HSENI, Planning Service and NIEA."

PLs - Petroleum licences, are issued by DETI, the Department for Enterprise, Trade and Investment.

But the anti-fracking movement received some consolation in December 2011 when the Northern Ireland Assembly passed a Green/Alliance motion supporting a moratorium on fracking, both onshore and offshore. The Minister for Enterprise, Trade and

Investment, Arlene Foster, told the Assembly that she supported the economic benefit fracking could bring, but paid lip service to objectors by saying that she recognised the validity of concerns and promising that applications would be subjected to the full rigour of the planning system and associated Environmental Impact Assessment Reports. She argued that a moratorium was not appropriate because at present no applications were granted or pending. She was also hoping that more studies, particularly from the US, would show the process to be safe. The vote, however, went in favour of a moratorium. Foster's DUP (Democratic Unionist Party) voted against.

Of the four companies with PL licences, the only one which is stating often and loudly that they are pursuing fracking is Tamboran. CEO Richard Moorman announced he was disappointed by the Assembly decision, because Tamboran's shale exploration activities are "100% safe".

Despite this seeming good news, Tamboran no doubt took comfort in the fact that no Northern Irish legislation exists to compel a minister to act upon a moratorium. Although promising to carry out more studies, pro-fracking Foster is able to ignore the Assembly vote.

Tamboran holds a substantial licence in both Northern Ireland and the Republic of Ireland, covering the Lough Allen Basin, found in parts of counties Leitrim, Roscommon, Sligo, Cavan and Donegal in the Republic, and Fermanagh in Northern Ireland. Tamboran is an Australian/Canadian company which promotes itself as "an innovative explorer for hydrocarbons in Australia and overseas".

In January 2012 the Financial Times reported Tamboran as saying they had discovered a gas field straddling the border of the Republic of Ireland and NI with potential reserves of 4.4 trillion cubic feet of gas. They estimated they could create a total of 1,200 jobs on both sides of the border. However, this estimate has to be viewed as total guesswork, since it was based only on desk studies of historical seismic and drilling data from other companies.

In April 2012 the publication of the UK government's report about seismological effects of fracking was met with some caution in NI. Environment Minister Alex Attwood pointed out that the earthquake question was the only one that had been addressed, and concerns about fracking extended far beyond that. Sinn Fein energy spokesman Phil Flanagan said that a review by the British Government was irrelevant, and called claims that fracking was safe "bizarre". Maybe he had the BBC's Northern Ireland report in mind, which was headed "Fracking for oil and gas 'safe' says report".

The Assembly's Green Party MLA (Member of the Legislative Assembly) Steven Agnew also criticised the report, saying: "This report has been unfortunately misinterpreted to suggest that fracking is a safe process - it is not." The Greens claimed that Tamboran's ambition was to drill 9,000 gas wells across Ireland.

In May 2012 the Belfast Telegraph reported that Tamboran was not the only fracking company which intended to make a move. DETI was prompted to respond to concern that Canadian firm Rathlin Energy Ltd was about to apply for fracking in its licence area, bounded by Garvagh, Magilligan and Ballycastle and extending to the north coast. Rathlin confirmed they were studying the results of surveys to inform their investment plan. DETI confirmed they had not submitted any application but refused to rule it out in the future.

Arlene Foster remained an unapologetic pro-fracker, despite the fact that she has come under criticism for failing to disclose her own financial interests in fracking, and it being subsequently found that her family owned potential fracking land in County Fermanagh. She subsequently revealed she had another interest in a different land holding. This was not the first time she has been involved in conflict of interest allegations. In Northern Ireland donations to political parties are kept secret, another concern for those who take a sceptical view of the DUP's pro-fracking stand.

When the UK government decision that fracking could resume was announced on 13th December 2012, this was countered in NI by environment minister Alex Attwood who said any decision regarding fracking should be left to Stormont. He went on to say that any forthcoming planning application would be decided by his department, as had been the case with other energy applications. Although this raises questions about local input to planning decisions in NI, Attwood went on to say:

"Renewables is arguably Ireland's biggest economic opportunity – electricity self sufficiency, net energy exporters, research and development jobs, engineering and manufacturing growth. We need to fully embrace this."

For Richard Moorman the pressure was too much. He resigned as CEO of Tamboran, but remained a technical advisor. He commented regarding the company's plans:

"The company's going in a bit of a different direction. They're aggressively pursuing a joint venture party for the Australian assets and so the company is essentially going slower in Ireland. It became impossible to keep the pace there."

Regarding the general European situation he said -

"The European experience so far has been frustrating.

"Certainly Cuadrilla in the UK, sitting on what appears to be a very viable asset, had the misfortune of setting off tremors on their first fracture stimulation and subsequently the report has come out that showed that there were steps they could take to prevent that from happening, but that's in the record."

Maybe Moorman lost his job because he hadn't achieved value for money. Tamboran's attempt to spend 20,000 euro persuading the Manorhamilton Enterprise Forum, a business forum, backfired. MEF planned to use the money to build a new hotel in Manorhamilton, over the border in Leirtrim. No Fracking Ireland and other groups deplored this buying of the local business community, particularly as they believed fracking ran counter to the aims of any tourism initiative.

This accepted bribe in May 2012 was followed by a report in the Irish Independent that Tamboran had a multi-million euro account set up to provide a "war chest" for "community donations".

In evidence given to the Northern Ireland Assembly's Committee for Enterprise, Trade and Investment in June 2012, the then CEO Moorman admitted that despite claims to being a "world class" global unconventional oil and gas exploration and development company, Tamboran had only 12 full-time and 10 part-time employees. Yet it holds rights and permits for more than 27 million acres across the world. Tamboran has *no* experience in drilling.

There are many detailed issues to be examined should Tamboran come up with a fracking proposal. Tamboran has stated that its fracking would use no chemicals, an odd claim. And, as another example, evidence submitted to DETI by the Fermanagh Fracking Awareness Network FFAN suggested that:

"In Fermanagh, there are two layers being pursued by Tamboran – the Bundoran Shale and the Dowra Sandstone. These geological formations are classified as Locally Important Aquifers, and are directly underlain by a Regionally Important Karstified aquifer and separated from an overlying Regionally Important Aquifer by ca. 400-600m of fractured shales and sandstones. Both the Regionally Important Aquifers are used as sources of water by public supplies. Numerous water-dependent protected areas are located within the area under study".

In January 2013 Tamboran's hopes for exploration were still quoted to be a year off.

For a country to place its countryside in the hands of Tamboran and expose its population to the hazards of fracking by a company which is nothing but a financial adventurer with no experience and substance would be incredibly foolish and blameworthy. But that is the way it may go if Arlene Foster has her way. And if people give any credence to the likes of PwC, who claimed on 14th February that there was an estimated £80 billion of gas under the north west and Fermanagh in Northern Ireland, a claim that Sinn Fein called "sensationalist".

23 Wales, CBM and UCG

Wales is an obvious target for would-be extreme energy producers as it still sits on top of large unexploited coal reserves.

At the beginning of September 2008 Eden Energy announced that they had completed test drilling in the Llynfi Valley near Bridgend and two other sites, Port Talbot and Pencoed. The tests revealed "huge quantities" of high quality CBM gas, according to the Guardian. The paper also reported some excitement at the news. Huw Irranca-Davies, MP for Ogmore in South Wales believed that people would be very supportive once they were aware of a "huge" potential.

Wyn Davies, clerk to two local community councils in the Llynfi Valley, repeated what Eden had told them, that just one seam of gas would power 1,000 homes for 100 years.

In 2005 Mr Irranca-Davies was advocating opening up mines in Wales again using "clean coal technology with zero emissions". Hmm. For a year or so until late 2011 he was Labour's Shadow Energy Minister. In February 2011 he reacted positively to a proposal by Coastal Oil and Gas to drill for gas in Llandow. He described the potential for job creation as "exciting". Irranca-Davies is frequently excited, according to press reports, whether it's about plans to expand RAF St Athan, or Caerphilly's Dracula Castle.

But it is difficult for him to avoid a charge of hypocrisy. Only weeks earlier he was praising the huge potential for shale gas, saying it could bring secure and more affordable gas, and endorsing the Llandow exploration, while as Shadow Minister he was calling for the government to apply a moratorium on test fracking in Lancashire. Hardly compatible with saying residents should not be concerned about a test borehole at Llandow.

The affair is a warning to opponents of fracking that a change of government, with Labour in power, is not likely to be the coming of the saviour.

In 2010 Wales Online reported that opposition was mounting to Centrica (which owns British Gas) plans to drill for gas in old coal beds. This resentment was in part due to the fact that Centrica had carried out surveying operations on land near Llangeinor without informing landowners, and had talked about the possibility of applying for a compulsory purchase order. The group, which acquired PEDL licences in 2008, said they had submitted three planning applications in the Ogmore Valley area. They pointed out that IGas had been successfully running a pilot scheme for two years generating electricity from CBM at Doe Green, near Warrington. As the well at Warrington had been fracked, it may be assumed that the Ogmore Valley wells could also be fracked.

More attempts to drill for gas started in the Vale of Glamorgan. In August 2011 Wales Online reported that Coastal Oil and Gas Ltd had resubmitted a planning application to the Vale of Glamorgan Council. They had withdrawn an earlier application, which raised objections because of the proximity of a private house to the proposed drilling site on the Llandow Industrial Estate.

Now Coastal were back, with a noise impact survey they claimed supported their case. Council planners recommended approval. Objectors were worried that the application would lead to a shale fracking operation. In a reverse twist of localism, Vale leader Gordon Kemp called for the application to be called in by the Welsh Government, as the application was said to be of national significance, but this did not happen.

Gerwyn Williams, CEO of Coastal, confirmed that the drilling would test the potential for fracking as well as for conventional gas resources. And the plans were to drill into shallow shales only some 500-600m below the surface, which is of course less than the recommended 600m minimum we have now come to see accepted as being required between shale and groundwater.

Vale MP Alun Cairns called for the Wales Government to handle all Welsh fracking applications. Assembly Member AM Jane Hutt objected to the plans.

By the following month, Williams was telling BBC Radio Wales that the application only concerned conventional gas, not shale. Coastal had attempted to fudge the shale issue by resubmitting plans which said that their target was not the shales but conventional sandstone oil or gas resources below the shale. It is believed, however, that these had been explored some 20 years earlier and been found non-viable.

In a news report he BBC also exposed the fact that documents published ahead of the Vale Council's planning committee meeting confirmed the sampling would include looking for fracking potential. They quoted from the planning report:

"The application is made by Coastal Oil and Gas Limited for the purpose (as defined in their submissions) of 'drilling to take core samples of limestone shales with a view to future possible capture and supply of shale gas (unconventional gas) as a clean energy supply and also to penetrate the Upper Devonian measures to test for the presence of conventional gas".

An examination of the report also reveals:

"The drilling is estimated to be to a depth of approximately 650m, and forms part of a continuing program of sampling across South Wales, permissions having previously been granted in Bridgend County Borough Council and Neath Port Talbot County Borough Council. The applicant advises that further applications are pending in both these areas and one is due to be submitted to Rhondda Cynon Taf Council.

In supporting information, the applicants advise that shale gas (natural gas produced from shale) is becoming an increasingly important source of gas in North America and potential resources exist in many other parts of the world."

The Vale councillors were clearly unimpressed. They voted unanimously to refuse the application. Coastal announced it was to appeal the decision, which had been made after Welsh Water said it believed there was a "very small risk" of contamination of its reserve groundwater sites from the proposed drilling.

It took until May 2012 for the Welsh Planning Inspectorate to hold a public enquiry, and it was July before they came to a decision on the Llandow application. Welsh Water had retracted on their earlier statement, after talks with Coastal, and now said in their opinion any water contamination risks were minimal. They refused to attend the appeal.

The Inspectorate overturned the local council decision and gave the application the go-ahead. Whilst the planning inspector Emyr Jones said that a significant number of objections had been raised on concerns about future fracking, no extraction or hydraulic fracturing was part of the application and he could not support those objections. He stressed that any future proposal for fracking would have to go through another planning exercise and should not be prejudiced by his decision. FoEC (FoE Cymru) disagreed, saying the floodgates had been opened to fracking in Wales.

Local MP Alun Cairns was reported as being "dismayed" by the decision. However he announced:

"We are all however delighted that the owner of the site, John Winslade of LEL properties and Ledley Engineering, had confirmed in his submission to the Inquiry that the terms of the lease do not permit drilling on the site and that he was not prepared to consider varying the terms of the lease".

FoEC had also recently reacted with dismay at a report that half of the Welsh population could be affected by shale gas drilling if proposed licences were issued in the 14th round of licensing. Whether the Llandow testing went ahead or not, the fear was there that a precedent had indeed been established.

In December 2012 Gerwyn Williams told the press that Coastal were still interested in the Llandow site, but had six more potential drilling sites. Meanwhile UK Methane Ltd had lodged application with Bridgend Council for three boreholes at a disused colliery site at Maesteg. Wearing his UK Methane hat, Williams repeated the line that the Maesteg application was not for fracking, but again refused to rule out future fracking at the site. The boreholes would only be between 130 and 300 metres deep.

Looking at the Bridgend County Borough Council's web site shows, in fact, that permission was granted to UK Methane to test drill at the former St Johns Colliery in April 2011. The application was to "drill and test the in situ Namurian Shale and associated strata". This flew beneath the radar of local Green party and other opposition. In the event the drilling appears to have failed.

However the October 2012 application was to "drill 3 boreholes to abandoned workings at St Johns Colliery & generate electricity". In other words a CBM production application.

Naturally the Westminster government's green light for fracking boosted new speculation. RPS group "renowned experts in shale gas" according to Wales Online, predicted Eden Energy's exploration licences could hold 34 trillion cubic feet of gas, of which 12.8 is classified as recoverable. This 38% recoverable figure will raise eyebrows even amongst fracking's supporters. This is an incredibly optimistic estimate to justify RPS saying the gas could be worth £120bn.

Eden Energy are the Australian company with a 50% stake in Coastal Oil and Gas Ltd.

Andy Chyba, chairperson of the Bridgend Green party, pointed out that in Wales there was significant fracturing below ground due to coal mining. Although as a geologist himself he had previously urged caution in expressing fears about seismic activity, he believed that seismic activity was a definite threat to the valleys of South Wales. He says:

"Even very modest seismic activity will destroy the integrity of well casings - cracking concrete and distorting steel."

In January 2013, when the UK Methane application for extracting coal bed gas at Maesteg was passed by Bridgend Council, Chyba did not hide his view of the decision and UK Methane, in a letter he sent to the Glamorgan Gazette and three other newspapers:

"The recent rubber-stamping of a relatively small scale Coal Bed Methane (CBM) planning application for the St Johns Colliery site in Maesteg needs to be seen in its full and proper context. The applicants in this case are UK Methane, who are the same few people as Coastal Oil & Gas, who have put through a similar small scale CBM project at Cwmcedfyw Farm, near Llangynwyd. The grandiose sounding names of these companies hide the fact they are tiny companies consisting of Mr

Gerwyn Williams and a couple of his mates. They do not own any resources; having to bring in Sunderland based contractors, Drillcorp, to drill at Cwmcedfyw, with labour picked up on route from Liverpool. These small scale projects are not really what they are about. It is a tactical approach used by the infamous Cuadrilla company in Lancashire, and other companies elsewhere. They undertake a couple of small, relatively innocuous methane projects (there are still serious issues over water contamination) to try and convince local people, and local planning departments, that they are not up to anything worth worrying about and that they can be trusted. With peoples guards down, they then sneak through applications for their real target shale gas that will require the use of the deep fracking techniques that have proven to be unreliable and the bringer of dire consequences (sooner or later, but inevitably) to local people and their environments.

Be under no illusion as to what Gerwyn and his cronies are up to. They are not very clever at disguising their intentions. Down at Llandow, their initial bungled application clearly stated shale gas at the target. As soon as the locals rose up and organised opposition (the Vale Says No! Campaign group) they resubmitted trying to pretend they were only really interested in conventional sandstone oil/gas. Pathetic. At St Johns Colliery, they successfully sneaked an application through to target the deep lying shales in January 2011, before we caught on to what they are up to. They again brought Drillcorp in to do that test borehole, but my understanding is that they had to abandon it because Drillcorp's equipment was not up to the job.

Gerwyn is getting on a bit. Speculating on unconventional gas is his pension plan, I believe. He has picked up licences to explore for resources for very little investment (just a few thousand pounds) in South Wales, the Mendips and Kent. By undertaking some test drilling and conjuring up fanciful figures for the potential resource, he will look to sell on his licences at substantial profit and disappear into the sunset well before the frackers roll in and wreak their havoc".

Meanwhile in Swansea test drilling for coal bed methane was also applied for at the Llys Nini Animal Centre in Penllegar. Swansea Council's planning committee passed the application, despite concerns from objectors and some councillors. This time the applicant was UK Methane. (Interestingly although the Maesteg application was in the name of Coastal Oil and Gas, some of the documentation refers to UK Methane. Perhaps Mr Williams sometimes forgets which hat he is wearing).

Sally Hayman, the chairwoman of the trustees of the Llys Nini Animal Centre, affiliated to the RSPCA and sporting their logo, claimed the charity was independently funded. However it is clear the RSPCA own the drilling site. They say there is the possibility that methane is leaking from the old coal workings below ground, and they are using UK Methane to find out more about what is happening underground, to see if the seepage problem can be solved.

However, protestors point out that the UK Methane proposals were for "drilling an exploration Coal Bed Methane borehole to 800-1000m". This would go far beyond the 300m at which depth old coal workings are known to exist - the probable source of any methane leak.

If this is purely to assist the RSPCA in the worthy aim of reducing fugitive methane emissions, why do UK Methane need to drill so deep?

UK Methane told the South Wales Evening Post that previous drilling in South Wales revealed very high quality gas reserves of some 90 to 98 per cent methane. It is hard to deny the suspicion that once again this is CBM extraction, possibly involving fracking, by stealth.

The RSPCA said, in their innocence:

"A planning application has been approved to allow a test bore hole to be drilled on our car park. This should tell us whether there is methane trapped in the coal measures below the site.

We will carefully consider the results of the drilling to see if the gas can be extracted without any damage to biodiversity on site, to the environment or nuisance to our neighbours.

Coal bed methane is not extracted by "fracking" or "gasification"."

Swansea is not only under attack by applications for potential CBM production - and granting test applications - but from energy companies intent on UCG exploitation.

In January 2012 the BBC reported that Clean Coal Ltd (a name which will draw hollow laughter from energy realists) confirmed it wanted to apply for permissions for UCG under Swansea Bay.

In their licence area they expected to find a billion tonnes of coal. They wanted to focus on finding an area of perhaps 30 to 50 million tonnes of coal that was suitable for UCG. CCL's executive chairman is Rohan Courtney. He is claimed in his press releases to be an energy industry "veteran". In reality he has a background in merchant banking and only set up an interest in UCG in 2005. Prior to that he was a non-executive director in Tullow Oil.

His company's press release to Wales Online stated that UCG is a "long-established technique", used in such places as Russia, China and South Africa.

Far from being an established technique, UCG is still in an experimental stage. Even DECC, which is in favour of encouraging UCG, can only say this:

"The basic feasibility of UCG has been proven in previous trials. Further detailed studies are required to prove the technology of precision drilling process control over sustained periods of operation and to fully evaluate any possible environmental impact on underground aquifers and adjacent strata. One of the practical problems of UCG is that meaningful experiments cannot be carried out in the laboratory, and trials must be undertaken at pilot scale, which is both costly and time consuming."

The population of Swansea might be excused for not wanting a potentially polluting technology to be trialled on their doorstep.

Even Clean Coal, when not pushing out press propaganda, admits that the technology has had its failures in terms of protecting groundwater or avoiding surface subsidence. As with shale gas, the justification for continuing trials of a hazardous procedure is that new knowledge and regulation will correct mistakes of the past. No trials have yet taken place in the UK or off the UK coastline. Courtney would do well to consider more deeply his ex-company Tullow's admission that "The oil and gas industry is inherently hazardous." And there is nothing more hazardous than a new untried untested technology.

Licences for UCG are issued by the Coal Authority. Partly for that reason the number of licences that have been issued for UCG has gone largely unreported. Over 20 have been granted around the coast of Britain between 2011 and 2013. The latest two are to Cluff Natural resources, for development in Wales off the Carmarthen coast, the Loughor Estuary project, and between Merseyside and North Wales in the Dee Estuary project.

Although the company's founder, Algy Cluff, claims extensive experience in the natural resource sector, it is as an investor. Indeed Cluff Natural Resources is purely an investment company. It is not clear what an investment company will do with its new licences. It has no experience in UCG, unsurprisingly. The Loughor and Dee estuary projects are its first acquisitions. This is yet another opportunistic company set up to make money out of buying and selling on exploration licences.

I am sure I am not alone in thinking this is a recipe for disaster. What on earth is the Coal Authority thinking of?

Part of the Loughor Estuary falls within the Gower area of outstanding natural beauty. All of it is within the Carmarthen Bay and Estuaries special conservation area, and close to Burry Inlet, a Ramsar site of international importance.

Frack Off describes risks of UCG as including those arising from toxic waste, waste disposal, air pollution, aquifer pollution subsidence, surface plant and power station blight and road traffic, citing mainly effects of UCG testing in Australia. Offshore UCG is currently untrialled and considered to be a more reckless attempt than shale gas fracking at scraping the bottom of the fossil fuel barrel. Proponents of UCG stress its benefits when combined with CCS. But without CCS we're back to the same old problem. Extreme energy fossil fuels can not be a bridge to a low-carbon future. It is just walking the plank.

24 Scotland

In Scotland unconventional gas plans advanced quietly for a number of years with exploration and testing, but the alarm bells didn't sound until Dart Energy made it clear that their Scottish CBM project, perhaps the most advanced in Europe, was targeting Airth in the Forth Valley. At the same time applications by Greenpark Energy - subsequently acquired by Dart, went ahead for another CBM project involving fracking in Canonbie in Dumfries and Galloway.

Again, as in Wales, perhaps, the environmental movement had seen the growing awareness of shale gas dangers, without realising the threat of CBM.

FoES (FoE Scotland) quickly diverted its energies to combating the CBM threat and raising public awareness of CBM issues.

This is not to say that shale gas fracking was not already an issue in Scotland. In May 2011 the Sunday Herald reported that an Australian company was about to apply for permission to drill the country's first shale exploratory well. Composite Energy, in fact, had become a wholly-owned subsidiary of Dart in February of that year, and in June was renamed Dart Energy (Europe) Ltd.

The test well was at Airth near Falkirk. It was said to be unfracked, bored down to 2,000m. The Scottish government sat on the fence, saying that unconventional gas offered huge potential as long as development was consistent with environmental objectives, a rather meaningless stance.

The owners of Composite, having sold their interest to Dart for £40 million, promptly set up a new company, Hutton Energy, in Glasgow, with the intention of floating for £60 million in 2012.

In November 2011 the Scottish Environmental Agency granted a licence to Greenpark to extract coal bed gas near Canonbie. Executive vice-president of Greenpark David Harper confirmed that they intended to frack at Canonbie and at a second site for which they wanted to lodge an application. Malcolm Roberts, a principal policy officer for SEPA, the Scottish Environmental Protection Agency, played down potential risks and said fracking was likely to become more widespread in coming years. The word was that "They are not high-risk operations provided they are done properly".

Dart Energy, having bought up Composite Energy and Greenpark Energy, was now Scotland's major player, with exploratory sites in Falkirk, Stirling, Clackmannanshire, Fife, and Dumfries and Galloway.

Another company, Dart Shale Ltd, was set up and shows considerable gas reserves on its books. Clearly, whatever they say, and whatever their planning permissions were for originally, Dart has a big interest in both CBM and shale.

By August 2011 Dart were confident enough to sign a £300 million five year deal with Scotia Gas Networks to sell them gas from their Airth CBM site, hoping for production to start the following year.

Two of the licences they took over from Greenpark were for fracking "into groundwater" in coal seams at Mouldyhills and Broadmeadows, near Canonbie. 26 planning applications led to permissions at 17 borehole sites. Near Airth SEPA had granted licences for 11 boreholes.

In August 2012 Dart submitted two planning applications to Falkirk and Stirling County Councils to build 14 new well pads with 22 new wells, around 20 km of pipelines to connect the sites, a gas processing facility and a waste outfall into the Firth of Forth, near Airth between Falkirk and Stirling. Their aim is to produce Coal Bed Methane (CBM) from coal seams around 850 metres below the farmland to the west of Airth. This would be the first serious unconventional gas development in the UK, which involves gas production rather than testing.

The difficulty for the public in addressing a large application like this is hinted at by the Falkirk application, which consists of no less than 125 documents. Nevertheless, to-date (early February

2013) over 500 public representations had been made. The Stirling application is smaller, with over 50 documents. Around 125 representations have been made.

Frack Off's summary of the application situation is this -

14 new and 2 existing well sites
22 new coal bed methane wells
About 20 km of pipelines
1 waste outfall into Firth of Forth
1 gas processing facility

And that there are plans for up to 600 more wells in the area, the beginning of a massive attack on the countryside.

In December 2012 the Scottish Herald voiced fears that the UK government's go-ahead for fracking meant a quarter of Scotland had been opened up to shale gas exploration, and reported that more than 20,000 square kilometres, or 7,800 square miles, had been "earmarked" for possible exploitation by controversial technologies such as fracking.

The Herald said that SEPA *"is tightening its regulation of unconventional gas extraction, and says that after April 2013, operators will be required to say what chemicals they want to use for drilling operations."*

Scotland, one can infer, lags even behind England in its regulatory control.

The Herald reported that Dart or its predecessors had already drilled at sites in Clackmannanshire, Fife and Dumfries and Galloway. Another company, Reach Coal Seam Gas, had a permission to explore at Cumbernauld.

Dart told the Herald that it believed underground gas to be clean, safe and cost-effective. It would boost the Scottish economy and reduce reliance on imported gas. Same old story.

Dart also said it had no plans to *frack* in Falkirk or Stirling, but admitted it had two fracking licences in coal seams in Mouldyhills and Broadmeadows. It wasn't intending to use them. How much this is worth in an industry where neighbourhoods are bought and sold depending on the energy industry's whim is clear. There are no promises. Once you have given permission, the permission is a simple commodity.

Newsnet Scotland ran the same story and commented that Dart's Australian website noted the potential of the Scottish sites, that Dart was facing opposition at home, and that its share price had fallen 72% after fierce opposition and negative publicity. It hadn't made a profit for two years, and plans to be listed on the Singapore and UK stock markets had been postponed. This raised questions about investor support, despite the fact that the Airth CBM project was prominent in the group's portfolio.

It is hard to believe that Scotland's interests are near the top of Dart's considerations. The country is being used as a pawn in an Australian company's international multi-million gambles.

Dart dragged in Chris Faulkner, chief executive of Breitling Oil and Gas in Texas, to support their pro-fracking argument. He said:

"The environmental impacts of fracking can be effectively curtailed through a combination of technology, innovation and smart regulation."

Unfortunately, Scottish regulation is not smart. Dart has already been pumping out waste from coal beds near Airth into the Firth of Forth since early 2012. According to Frack Off, Freedom of Information requests resulted in the disclosure that the SEPA had performed no tests on the waste, and any tests had been carried out by Dart themselves. Dart's discharge permission, which they inherited (and which were granted in 1997 before newer regulation came into effect) is for 300,000 litres per day. Their new planning applications are a substantial expansion of their current Airth testing site.

Breitling Oil and Gas is another new company that makes its money from promoting the industry rather than being a player.

"Breitling Oil and Gas was founded in October 2004 to apply state-of-the-art petroleum and natural gas exploration and extraction technology to the development of onshore oil and natural gas projects. Our focus areas include Texas, Oklahoma and Louisiana. Breitling offers oil and gas investment opportunities through direct participation programs and oil and gas investment joint ventures which enable investors to participate in the potential cash flow and unique tax benefits associated with oil and

gas investments. Especially important in a downturned economy, oil and gas investments allow savvy investors to diversify and reinforce their investment portfolios with a stable commodity that is in steady demand."

I am sure savvy Scots can tell hype when they hear it. But I am not so sure they can distinguish, as I can't without looking at endless detail, between an application for CBM extraction, as distinct from a fracking application. This is an increasing problem. The industry is able to take advantage of the opposition to shale gas fracking, in order to promote their applications for other equally undesirable technology. In other words, if they say their application is not for "fracking", they are more likely to reduce objection and get an application passed, despite the fact that with CGM, alternative technologies, particularly extraction of water contained within the coal seams, may be even more dangerous than fracking. This is the serious danger of making "fracking" a dirty word.

After the announcement that the UK government was to give the go-ahead to fracking, there was the expected combination of responses.

Labour Member of the Scottish Parliament Graeme Pearson said:

"Few people in Scotland can avoid the high costs of heating their homes. The US has seen gas costs fall to 1990 levels in the last five years thanks to fracking."

A commentator on this remark as reported in the Daily Record said:

"Fracking appears to be toxic, environmentally and for people, and irreversibly landscarring. And all Graeme Pearson can do is have a pop at the SNP?

"Thanks for that valuable contribution to the complex issue of affordable fuel. I'm sure any of your constituents who drink water or breathe air will be delighted with it."

25 Regulation

It is always possible that the fracking companies may withdraw, in the face of the new opinions and evidence appearing regularly now that suggest the shale bubble is about to burst, that shale gas can never be economic in Europe. It is possible that further exploration will convince the shale frackers that the pickings will not be as rich as their investors demand. Looking on the dark side, it is also possible that a major accident will persuade the government to halt fracking.

But until there is any evidence of this happening, the main way the frackers will be stopped is by public opposition, making fracking an untenable proposition for not only the frackers but the government.

Some opponents of fracking argue that the only way to prevent an environmental disaster is a complete onshore ban, and that regulation is a red herring. Others, whilst agreeing in principle, believe that the question of regulation is too important to ignore. Pro-frackers say, and maybe this is currently a majority belief amongst the general public, is that fracking will be safe if we have adequate regulation and enforcement. We're British, after all, and surely our safeguards will be the best in the world. Would it were so.

The argument that regulation will save us fails for two reasons. One, the evidence so far is that the government has no intention of imposing restrictive regulation which would deter the gas industry, or admitting that a complete overhaul of the regulatory agencies and their funding is necessary. Two, that the best regulation in the world will not prevent human error, accidents, and the long-term inevitable failure of wells.

In England a number of bodies are involved in potential regulation of fracking. These are DECC, HSE, the EA, the Minerals Planning Authorities (read county councils) and also for CBM, particularly, the Coal Authority, a part of DECC.

The government-commissioned report, by the Royal Society and Royal Academy of Engineers, raised doubts about whether these bodies were sufficiently coordinated for the challenges that shale gas exploitation presents. They also raised doubts about adequacy of funding. But most importantly, they stated quite clearly that current regulations are inadequate to regulate shale gas.

The regulations in force essentially date back to coal mining regulation. Later the law was amended to take account of North Sea Gas. What we have is an outdated hotchpotch, ill-equipped to cope with onshore shale gas development. The HSE experience is almost entirely with offshore wells. They have neither the finance nor the staff to adequately police onshore exploration. DECC and the EA are similarly ill-equipped to deal with onshore shale gas problems. They are on a learning curve, and without experience coming from the UK, they are reliant on desk work, and the assistance of oil industry co-workers. If shale gas production really gets going in the UK, the regulators will be learning on the job. This is bad news for the public and for the environment.

However, it is quite clear that the government, whilst talking about regulation, is in a cleft stick. It has already claimed that UK regulation is quite adequate. However even its experts now say it is not fit for purpose. Yet the government will not want to fund extensive research into what is required for two reasons - firstly the expense, and secondly the rush to exploit shale gas led by the chancellor for economic and "energy security" reasons. The urgency is compounded by the fact the government's policy on renewables is in tatters. Indeed it is not unfair to say its whole energy policy is in disarray, and every part of the energy sector, whether wind, solar, nuclear or shale, is complaining at the indecision the government is displaying regarding its intentions.

The first indication that the government was unwilling to implement major reforms in onshore oil and gas exploration came in 2011, in the response to the report from the Environment and Climate Change Committee. Two major examples of how the government failed to respond to its own MPs' concerns were regarding abandonment of wells and waste disposal.

The Committee was concerned about contaminated and abandoned sites, and recommended that a fund should be established to ensure that if a well were abandoned it could be plugged. An upfront bond or a levy on shale gas well drilling was suggested.

The government failed to see the point that was also missed by the committee, that it is not a question of operators being required to plug wells before abandonment, but who is going to monitor and pay for well failure - which is inevitable at some time - in the future. The government's response to the committee's concern was that no further powers are necessary. It only referred to controls in existence to provide remedy for environmental problems *prior* to site surrender.

The Committee also recommended that UK legislation should take specific account of the challenges unique to shale gas exploration and production, and in particular to the large volumes of waste water that must be managed and disposed of. The government replied using the industry line that the technologies used in shale gas are not "generically novel or unfamiliar". Hydraulic fracturing, water injection and lateral drilling, individually or in combination, were all familiar techniques that DECC and the other regulators have had to deal with robustly for a long time. So again, no need for new regulation, regarding waste water in particular,

"HSE feels that existing health and safety legislation (especially the regulations that address well design, construction integrity and control) already takes specific account of the challenges unique to shale gas exploration and production".

And:

*"The EA and SEPA (*Scottish Environment Protection Agency*) do not foresee significant challenges for wastewater treatment and disposal that are unique to unconventional gas activities. Operators will either transfer wastewater offsite for treatment to a permitted facility, or treat and dispose of wastewater onsite for which they will require an environmental permit themselves. Provisions for the safe handling of wastewater onsite will be a condition of local authority planning permission, and will be considered during the respective environment agencies' assessment of a site's environmental permitting requirements."*

Regarding the content of waste fracking fluid the government said:

"The environment agencies do not routinely monitor the chemical content of return fracking fluid or produced water from unconventional gas operations if it is not being disposed of directly to the environment. However, it will be necessary for operators to undertake their own analysis to allow them to dispose of waste fracking fluid via an appropriate waste management route (disposal off site)."

In other words, they confirmed the fears that this is in many ways a self-regulating industry.

"The environment agencies do not monitor air quality at unconventional gas operations.

"Local authorities also have a statutory duty under the Government's Air Quality Strategy and Local Air Quality Management process to monitor and assess local air quality."

It should be apparent that local authorities do not have the experience of (nor the funding) to monitor large scale industrial process of shale gas. Again, the government says that no new regulation is needed - another refusal on their part to accept the advice of their own committee and experts.

The Royal Society is a respected organisation. Even Lord Browne was once a president. The Society, together with the Royal Academy of Engineering, another prestigious body, was asked to look at shale gas, and they produced their report in June 2012.

The working party which produced the report included Professor Richard Selley, whom we have met before, and who is billed in the Royals' report as shale gas consultant to the Crown

Estate Commissioners. Other members of the party who had interests in the energy industry through consultancy and directorship included Dr Dougal Goodman, an ex General Manager at BP in charge of safety, Dr John Roberts, a chairman of Halite, the company proposing the scheme for an underground gas storage facility in the Fylde, Professor Zoe Shipton, who had been employed as consultant by amongst others BHP Billiton (one of the companies Francis Egan worked for), and Professor Paul Younger, a director of Five-Quarter Energy Limited, which champions the extraction of coal gas in the UK.

The reporting committee held eight evidence sessions, carried out numerous other consultations and received other written submissions.

An independent review panel was set up and commented on the report before it was approved by the RAE's Engineering Policy Committee and the Royal Society's Council. Members of both bodies were asked to declare potential conflicts of interest, and the report noted that both the RS and the RAE held their investments in portfolios including equity holdings in oil and gas companies.

In view of the above, we might have expected the government to have treated the report with all due seriousness, and listened to what recommendations the report made.

Unsurprisingly, when the report appeared it was greeted by the press as approving of shale gas.

"Fracking safe with strong regulation, report says" was the BBC report headline.

"UK fracking should be expanded, but better regulated, says report" was the Guardian's take.

"David Cameron's shale gas lifeline" said Telegraph blogger James Delingpole, a rabid journalist given to issuing gross insults and a climate change denier.

"Fracking should go ahead in Britain, report says" was the official Telegraph view.

"Engineers say UK fracking should proceed with caution. Shale gas needs strict monitoring but risks of water pollution and earthquakes have been overblown, study says." announced Business Green.

It is clear even from the headlines of most of the press articles that the report was not an unconditional go-ahead for fracking.

Inevitably, a detailed look through the report itself reveals a number of issues of concern that did not necessarily make it into even the report's own summaries but record the inadequacy of current regulation.

The government's response via DECC to the Royals Report was published on the 10th December 2012, just before the announcement that shale gas exploration could move ahead.

The response commented on the ten main recommendations of the report. Where there were positive proposals, for example the need for baseline testing to detect groundwater contamination, the reply failed to establish what contaminants should be included. And, curiously, the work of BGS with the EA to establish a national baseline would *exclude* Lancashire!

But generally it is the same old story. Self-regulation. Suggestions that DECC will require companies to put up information on their websites. Regarding abandoned wells DECC say this is a matter for the industry. Hardly adequate for the Fylde, which already has two failed and abandoned wells.

DECC ignores calls for well inspectors to be truly independent. They say regarding well design UKOOG (the UK Onshore Operators Group which has recently been revitalised to enhance the profile of the frackers) will establish good practice standards.

DECC would also seek UKOOG's guidance in how to monitor for leaking gas, and what constitutes good practice in water and waste management, and risk management. DECC says Environmental Risk Assessments will be expected to carry these out as good practice. A pliable arrangement with no binding guidelines.

Anybody who hasn't been persuaded by now that DECC is in the hands, if not the pocket, of the oil and gas industry must surely have serious doubts about the integrity of the government's position.

Royals recommendation:

"Mechanisms should be put in place to allow the reporting of well failures, as well as other accidents and incidents, between operators. The information collected should then be shared to improve risk assessments and promote best practices across the industry."

Response: *"There is already a range of mechanisms for well operators to share lessons from wells incidents, ranging from the global OGP Wells Expert Group to the UK Well Life Cycle Practices Forum and Oil & Gas UK and UKOOG. However, these fora have a much wider remit than just shale gas wells, so DECC will discuss this with the shale gas industry and ascertain the most appropriate routes to share best practice across shale gas operators."*

Indeed these fora have a wider remit than shale gas. They are industry organisations. OGP is the International Oil and Gas Producers Association. The UK Well Life Cycle Practices Forum was set up by OGP and as of mid 2012, the WLCPF had over 45 Oil & Gas UK member companies including operators and well management companies. OGP UK is as they themselves say "the voice of the offshore (sic) industry". They say:

"Our aim is to strengthen the long-term health of the offshore oil and gas industry in the United Kingdom by working closely with companies across the entire sector, governments and other stakeholders to address the important issues."

DECC reject setting up new funding for training within the regulatory bodies. In response to the Royals' statement of the need for more research, DECC say:

"The Research Councils are planning a workshop to consider the implications for UK research of the potential exploitation of unconventional hydrocarbon resources, including shale gas."

A workshop is the best response the government can come up with? With this final comment it is transparent that the serious concerns of the Royals Report have been brushed aside with a disregard verging on contempt.

To be fair, DECC did set up new regulations to try and prevent more earthquakes. But, tucked away at the back of the report into seismology for DECC is Appendix B. The comments there start with:

"In addition to the review report there is a general need to identify what should be done for future hydraulic fracture operations and general onshore drilling operations to be executed satisfactorily. Offshore operations have a well developed best practice regime but as there has been less onshore development, there is less in the way of protocols developed by bodies such as Oil and Gas UK."

There follows a list of 11 points considered necessary for best practice. These are unrelated to seismology, and mainly express concern about possible water pollution.

So even DECC's seismology report panel of experts felt it necessary to go outside their brief to comment on the fact that existing regulations were considered inadequate for onshore development, and there is also the clear implication that the industry's own guidelines were not adequate. Self-regulation will not work.

In summary, it has to be repeated that despite all the expert advice from two specialist reports that the government itself commissioned, and advice from its own committee of MPs, the only single point that was taken up by the government was a measure intended to calm public disquiet about the earthquake risk from fracking.

This is a woefully inadequate response. If shale gas production goes ahead, we are facing a high risk process operating with self-regulation by the operating companies with extremely limited oversight by enfeebled regulators.

26 The insider view

Since I considered my own layman's reaction to the Royals Report and the government's treatment of it, Mike Hill has given me a wealth of information on his own submissions to the study and his reaction. Frankly, I am now more concerned than I was before, if that is possible. I am now convinced that no amount of regulation will make fracking safe.

Mike Hill is a Chartered Engineer, and has worked in the oil and gas industry. He has been working on fracking regulation for the last two years. He has spoken at a number of gas conferences, including IGEM at Durham. He was technical advisor to the Fylde Borough Council for their shale gas Task and Finish group. He has since advised groups concerned about fracking in the Fylde, where he lives, particularly RAFF (Residents Action on Fylde Fracking) and REAF (Ribble Estuary Against Fracking), on technical matters.

Hill has met Cuadrilla representatives, particularly Mark Miller, on numerous occasions. Hill has given evidence to DECC, the Royal Society and Royal Academy of Engineers, and to Lancashire Council elected members. The Royal Society published Hill's evidence on their web site and included a number of his recommendations in their own report they presented to parliament.

Hill was disillusioned when he first started investigating the regulators' approach to onshore fracking. At first he expected the agencies to be clued up. But he was soon disabused. He says he found them breathtakingly complacent and/or incompetent, having never had to deal with onshore gas - a serious charge which is worth examining in more depth.

Hill has liaised frequently with members of the regulatory bodies. He has met DECC's head of Shale Gas on four occasions in Whitehall. Naturally Simon Toole disagreed with him regarding the need for onshore regulations. However Hill claims Toole did agree that the inspection regime was "non-existent". Hill also claims that HSE, although they visited Cuadrilla's well site in March 2011, have performed no well integrity testing. Hill says as an oil and gas engineer he knows that such testing is absolutely vital to ensure no contamination of the aquifers and groundwater by methane contamination or fracking chemicals, and to minimise fugitive emissions.

When the government gave permission for the resumption of fracking, they announced that they would set up a new body, the Office for Unconventional Gas. Its purpose would be to ensure a "simplified and streamlined regulatory process".

This has been perceived, however, as nothing more than a one-stop shop for investors in the industry.

Mike Hill says that he has spoken to the new head of the Office. Hill reports a heated discussion on the fact (as Hill sees it) that apart from the new regulations on seismicity, there are no specific regulations on shale gas, and no inspection regime. Hill spoke on two occasions to John Hayes and describes the minister as having extremely poor knowledge of what regulations there were in existence, what were needed, and indeed about fracking itself and how it is executed onshore. After educating Hayes, Hill says he was disappointed to find that both Hayes and DECC failed to take the opportunity to regulate the industry properly before allowing it to continue. In a letter to Hill, the minister quoted from Cuadrilla's website to try and inform Hill of what was happening. Hill finds this astonishing. Many readers who have stuck to the story so far will be less surprised. Yet another instance of decision makers or regulators taking all their facts as gospel from the fracking companies themselves.

Mike Hill's response to the RS&RAE report compares the report's recommendations with the evidence he gave to the working party at the request of chairman Professor Robert Mair. Hill was encouraged by the way the RS&RAE had taken up many of his points. His conclusion reads as follows:

"I feel that the RS and RAE have taken on aboard a lot of the points I have raised with them in my evidence. This is excellent and I am

delighted that after eighteen months of studying this industry and its regulation the other "authorities" and professional bodies are now adopting a lot of what I have been calling for over that time period.

"I trust now my argument, which was initially rejected by the authorities (DECC, HSE and EA), for additional onshore regulations and a significant tightening up of the U.K. procedures is now accepted by all. I have made it clear what those regs should be and the RS are very much in agreement. The key issue now is implementation. We urgently need a vehicle for delivering this regulation and ensuring it is implemented on the ground. This will require a considerable increase in resources and personnel. I have discussed this with the industry and it can be achieved with no cost to the taxpayer.

"I feel that it is important to have such measures in place not just before development but prior to the industry being give the go ahead to continue the exploratory phase. Three more wells will be fracked in 10 -12 multi-stage fracks in Lancashire. These are very close to urban conurbations and we need protection now not later. I urge the DECC to discuss this matter with myself and other stake holders so that we can get this structure fully in place prior to any development phase and underway prior to the commencement of fracking in the U.K."

Naturally Hill was disappointed that fracking was allowed the go-ahead with no extra regulation beyond the seismic traffic light system, and no extra resources funding the possibility of adequate monitoring of what regulations there are. I am sure also that the Royals started wondering why they went to all the trouble of conducting an investigation when their advice fell largely on deaf ears.

An issue which has not been raised elsewhere in this book is that of subsidence. The reason it has avoided mention so far is that the concern has not received widespread coverage. Indeed Mike Hill has suffered abuse for raising the issue from, amongst others, Mike Stephenson of BGS.

Hill took up this issue when he reviewed a paper on the subject by R J Stephenson in May 2012. R J Stephenson is a retired physicist with a subsidiary qualification in geology, and is now a resident of Lytham.

R J Stephenson's report considers the potential land subsidence as the result of fracking.

He examines the suggestion that the post-fracking compressibility of the shale beds will be greater after fracking than before, and that this then could lead to compression of the beds by pressure of the overlying strata. This could possibly lead to a lowering of the height of the land surface.

His conclusion is that if the government were to allow shale gas fracking to go ahead, this issue requires independent research. He recommends that before any fracking goes ahead, arrangements should be put in place to make provision for compensation to damage to buildings and infrastructure, including raising of sea defences, and that there should be a complete ban on any fracking on land less than 100m above sea level at high spring tide, below important structures such as nuclear installations, and below land where surface geography indicates the possibility of lake formation.

The British Geological Survey have refused to do any tests (the reason suggested being that they are too busy with testing depositing nuclear into shales and using shales for CCS).

Hill makes a pointed remark that in the 1920s the BGS stated that coal mining was very unlikely to cause subsidence.

Hill has come under attack for mentioning subsidence in public. Professor Mike Stephenson of BGS told a pro-fracking industry conference that there was "no foundation whatsoever to this. It simply won't happen. It's ridiculous."

Cuadrilla were pleased to put up an animated video on their web site including Professor Stephenson's remarks.

In the video Stephenson goes on to look at climate change and other areas outside his sphere of competence, and says "I am arguing that science needs to take a stronger role… we need more independent research, particularly independent science, to assess the risk, and to do it publicly and transparently… to talk about things we don't have to worry about, like Blackpool disappearing under the Irish Sea."

It isn't hard for anybody to see this was a chunk of hypocrisy, coming from a man who had simply brushed off Mike Hill's bringing the subsidence report to his attention and who had refused to consider any research.

Hill was understandably upset at the video attack, and in a strongly-worded email asked Mike Stephenson for more balance and reality, and described the video as propagating myths and having serious omissions.

Hill is not the only one to object to Mike Stephenson's pro-fracking and rather self-seeking stance. Here's a report from a previously non-aligned observer at a lecture at Lancashire University. The concluding remarks (again this evidence argues against the absurd notion that all concerned about fracking are crazy zealots) were these:

"I had understood that the lecture would cover resource size and impacts of extraction – it didn't really do either of those aspects, resource size clearly being a closely guarded secret and impacts of extraction really should also have included traffic, chemicals, the industrialisation of the sites, high volumes of water use etc.

"Overall I am glad I went, it was very interesting and I learned a lot from the lecture.

"The professor was an excellent lecturer, engaging with the audience, making them laugh at the thought of volcanoes occurring here and taking them down the road that shale gas is safe and a good thing...I feel the audience would wake up the next day 'knowing' that there were no issues of subsidence, no issues of radiation, no issues of earthquakes, it was a tried and tested technique and wow – it helps us achieve our climate change commitments too – so how could anyone reasonably object?

"However the geology of shale gas is just one small part of the shale gas business, the engineering and regulatory aspects have a huge influence on the risks and environmental effects, and that was not made at all clear. I did not feel that the Professor's lecture was truly balanced, rather that it was slanted to promoting the government's line"

If Stephenson and the industry he is unashamedly promoting believe smooth talking and good presentational skills will be enough to deceive the public they will be in for disillusionment, on this evidence.

Here is another thought from someone who attended the same lecture:

"Prof MS is a very smooth operator – we all came away with the same thought. But although he seemed very knowledgeable and reassuring during his lecture, I think the questions from the audience completely exposed him – I don't think there was a single question that he answered adequately, and that must have been very clear to everyone in the audience."

The next day Stephenson said in a Lancaster radio interview:

"What we are doing is a baseline study of natural water in water wells. The idea is to find out what the condition of the water is before anything happens – I mean nothing may happen but if it does we can be sure of what the original condition of water was, so that if for example, if there's a problem, let's say you know a company is extracting shale gas and there's a problem with the water then we'll know quickly and we'll be able to trace it to the activities so this is a kind of check if you like on what's going on"

To quote Refracktion, a Fylde commentator on Fylde fracking, *"We have to wonder whether the Professor is actually aware that one of his colleagues has stated publicly that the baseline study will **not** include Cuadrilla's sites in Lancashire."*

Rob Ward said:

"The British Geological Survey's (BGS) study to establish levels of methane in groundwater in the UK will not include sites 'fracked' by Cuadrilla Resources in Lancashire."

The question needs answering - why?

I suspect we know the answer very well. The BGS will accept Cuadrilla's data as gospel. It will incorporate these in its own estimates for shale gas resources. BGS and Cuadrilla are working hand-in-glove.

Mike Hill has recently (February 2013) lodged his further objections to Cuadrilla's applications to the EA for waste disposal. The applications were held until the outcome of the government's consideration of whether to allow shale gas exploration to continue, and the six applications covering Cuadrilla's three sites (one for fracking waste and one for radioactive waste at each site) were given an extended consultation period.

Hill states that the EA feels the public have not been given sufficient information in order to inform objections. This puts them at a disadvantage, especially as the EA holds information that they have withheld from the public by request of Remsol Limited (a company now employed by Cuadrilla as consultants for their waste disposal plans).

I am not, of course, sure what this information consists of, but it is a disturbing allegation, particularly in the light of all we have heard about how fracking companies have withheld information in the US, claiming company confidentiality.

Equally disturbing is what Hill says about the disposal of another type of waste, not the fracking flowback, but the cuttings and other materials that come up with the mud used in drilling. Hill says the EA simply describe it as saline. Maybe it is. But Hill has been on rigs where nobody would go near the mud without a full protective mask and suit.

The mud is returned with added components from the drilling. It should require checking before dumping. But the EA told Hill that they weren't responsible for checking, Cuadrilla were. The mud could contain mercury, chromium and a host of other waste elements. But nobody knows.

Despite this, Cuadrilla are allowed to dump their mud in municipal waste centres, which in the Fylde means Lytham. Hill says he personally is glad he does not live near Saltcoates Road. And it is extremely unlikely that anyone at Fylde Borough Council's tips knows about fracking waste.

More is known about the composition of the returned fracking fluid. Hill states in his objections to Cuadrilla's disposal plans that on certain dates it contained according to the EA (in comparison with mains water) -

90 times the permissible level of NORM (Naturally Occurring Radioactive Material)

1438 times the level of lead

150 times the level of cadmium

2,297 times the level of bromide

636 times the level of chromium

197 times the level of aluminium

20 times the level of arsenic

Hill states this is a fair comparison because that is a published result by the EA itself.

He asserts that well integrity is not checked by the EA or the HSE. And that the EA does not therefore have the knowledge of whether integrity has been compromised or not. It follows that it is wrong for fracking waste, which comes from perhaps a mile or two underground, to be compared with and classified as a standard industrial waste from a fixed plant. It is a potentially hazardous waste and should be treated as such.

Hill has asked the EA the following questions regarding Cuadrilla's application -

How will it be treated?

Where will it be treated ?

Who is treating it?

Where is it being disposed?

He has received no answers to any of these questions. The answer he got back was that this was "commercially sensitive information".

Hill asks how on earth can anyone object to an application or make representations when we do not have access to such information. The system is "ridiculous" in Hill's view. I would go further. I would say it is verging on the criminal.

A current issue that Hill is pursuing is the concern about well integrity failure. This is an important issue. Even the industry can not claim that wells do not have the ability to pollute water. They can argue that "fracking" has not been scientifically proven to pollute groundwater, but they have been unable to deny there is anecdotal evidence that taken together, the whole operation has the ability to pollute. In the UK we have the lack of regulation and law covering well construction, inadequate test methods for well failure, the lack of any regulatory body procedure, staff or funding to test, and the loss of any interest by regulatory bodies when a well has been abandoned and "signed off".

Hill says that the purpose of the visit by HSE to inspect Cuadrilla's well sites was only to look at worker H&S issues. Checking whether workers are wearing hard hats and safety goggles (as reportedly was the onsite check HSE made in March 2011) is not the same as checking other issues like well integrity. HSE have carried out other visits, but only to Cuadrilla's offices to look at paperwork.

HSE don't trust Cement Bond Logs and have no interest in inspecting them, and certainly not in carrying them out. Since Hill publicly criticised them for this they changed their stance a little, but Hill maintains that their approach and view is fundamentally flawed. CBLs may not be needed on multiple casing wells as long as CBLs are run for each cement job. Relying on annular pressure tests, as HSE insist is adequate, is simply not enough. Leakage up outside the casings due to progressive channelling will not be detected by AP, therefore the methane can migrate upwards.

HSE in any event rely entirely on what Cuadrilla feeds them. In practice HSE did not even ask for a CBL for their surface casing. Mike Hill did. HSE continues to avoid taking responsibility and shifts it to the operator, by suggesting receipt of a weekly fax at 3.15 on a Friday afternoon is the same as proper review and monitoring of drilling activity and well construction.

As we can see for ourselves from their website, HSE's guidance for well casings refers to regulations included in the Offshore Installation and Wells (Design and Construction etc) Regulations 1996. With its talk about offshore wells and underwater issues, clearly this needs revision.

In fact HSE say themselves:

"Health and safety law in Great Britain is goal setting and not prescriptive, there is no law stating how wells are cased and cemented. However the law states that employers, well operators, borehole operators must reduce risks to the health and safety of people from their operations to "as low as is reasonably practicable" (ALARP). This means they must follow good industry practice so that they can robustly demonstrate to HSE via the well notification that risks are ALARP."

So there are no legal standards, and it is left to operators to draw the line between what is technically feasible and what is economically acceptable to themselves.

This is no way to control a high-risk industry, particularly onshore where the reduction of environmental risk and health protection are paramount.

Frankly, those who still believe fracking is possible without risk are whistling in the wind.

As the state of regulation stands now, Mike Hill sums it up in one short sentence.

"We are not protected."

But the best regulation in the world can not *eliminate* risk. It can never eliminate human error. It will not change the fact that developing shale gas will exacerbate our climate change crisis. Onshore high-risk fossil fuel pursuit calls for only one solution, in my opinion, an absolute, unconditional and immediate ban.

27 Where do we go from here?

In the light of the fact that the UK government seems hell-bent on pursuing shale gas regardless of the consequences, with little or no regard to the concerns of either the public or its prestigious consultee experts, it would be tempting to think that the battle against fracking is lost.

This plainly is not a view shared by fracking's opponents. And there is every reason to think that opposition to fracking will continue to grow.

When Cuadrilla made their initial applications in the Fylde, there was little awareness of what they were seeking to achieve, and their planning applications were approved more or less on the nod and without the public, or even local councils being aware of the consequences. Sadly the success of these applications has prejudiced the situation. There is precedent set, however much local politicians may deny it.

The question is, a couple of years on, how best to tap the new awareness of the dangers fracking can and will cause, and how best to mobilise opposition.

Opposition did not, as has been suggested, spring up because of the injection into the Fylde of hard-line ecowarriors out to pursue their extreme interests.

The opposition in the Fylde has come in the main from local residents who began to realise how fracking could affect them and wanted to pass that realisation on to others. Some of them came to see the threat only when their peace and homes came under attack by Cuadrilla's geophysical survey.

The fact that fracking opposition there has not unified yet and produced a single body with widespread support and a focussed strategy is evidence of this. Of course the Green Party was in on the act early, but the Blackpool and Fylde Greens do not yet have a strong effective presence.

Today it seems that groups and web sites like RAFF, REAF (the main two residents' action groups), Refracktion and Frack Free Fylde have still not the central coordination that has been shown elsewhere, particularly in Somerset. This is something Lancashire campaigners will have to address.

Personally, I think a close look is needed at the realities of political life, and whether becoming involved in the political process should be one arm of the strategy. It may be that at the next County Council elections (due in May 2013) candidates running on an anti-fracking ticket would not have been elected. But an attempt should have been made, at the very least to take advantage of the opportunity which an election provides to raise public interest in a political issue.

Even if the idea of political opposition is rejected, there is a lesson to be learned from how experienced campaigning groups and political parties mobilise public support. This includes the desirability and method of leafleting, and frequent involvement with the press through personal approach and regular press releases.

No matter how the industry and the pro-fracking lobby may claim otherwise, fracking *is* a political issue. Not in a party-political sense necessarily, although clearly the Green Party is the only one of the parties with parliamentary and local representation to be relied on to give a consistent view. The Liberal Democrats have shown they will put aside their environmental principles and have been led into fracking by Ed Davey. It was always to be expected that the Conservatives would respond in a positive way to an industry lobby. As for the Labour party, their intentions regarding fracking will remain unclear until or unless they regain office.

At local political level, however, party members are at their most vulnerable. There is nothing more powerful in changing a councillor's view than the fear of losing his or her seat at the next election. This is something the anti-fracking lobby has yet to realise. Standing on the sidelines of the electoral system, wringing your hands while you try and raise public awareness is not enough. It is not the way to counter the strong forces which promote fracking.

Maybe in Lancashire there is a greater role to be played in coordination of local groups by experienced campaigners like Friends of the Earth. There are signs that this is now (February 2013) happening with, for example, FoE Manchester organising a training day on how to object to fracking planning applications. Maybe the situation is different on the ground in Lancashire from Somerset, where a wide coalition has formed to oppose fracking with unity and strength. But this needs analysis and if necessary a rethink.

As noted earlier, Cuadrilla have employed PPS, a company whose reputation is not spotless, to manage their PR.

The strategy involves not only a charm offensive but buying social acceptance.

In June 2011 Cuadrilla paid £500 to Elwick's Britain In Bloom campaign. Nine months later they gave £2,000 to Weeton Village Hall.

In January 2013 they gave £6,000 to the Snows Rebuilding Programme, via the (Lytham) Windmill Youth Development Group, which "specialises in creating future team leaders and managers in Commerce, World Affairs, The State Sector and Voluntary Bodies". Windmill organiser Stuart Sykes told his flock that on the 16th January "We also have a presentation at 7pm to the HSE UK Director of Cuadrilla who made a donation of £6000 to financially support Snows Heights. A donation for which we are most grateful." Snows Heights is an outdoor centre run by a charity of which Sykes is a trustee.

The next day, January 17th, Sykes wrote a letter to Lancashire County Council in support of Cuadrilla's planning application to horizontally drill at Anna's Road, going against the tide of the other eighty responses which opposed the application.

Also in January Cuadrilla engaged the local newspaper in publicising and promoting a Young Engineers Competition. This would involve local schools competing for £12,000 prize money.

This isn't the first time an energy company has infiltrated schools in order to impress the merits of the industry on young minds. BP is a "leader" in this field. But Cuadrilla's is a very blatant attempt to target a local community.

I also believe that unless a positive and well-planned strategy is employed by fracking opponents there will be no option but to resort to direct action and civil disobedience. Already I judge this as an appropriate alternative - or addition - to more conventional means of political and community opposition and lobbying.

It remains to be seen whether the recent determination by EDF to take civil action against the protestors who for a short while occupied the new gas station being built at West Burton in Nottinghamshire will backfire on the company. In February 2013 EDF launched a lawsuit seeking 5 million pounds in damages from No Dash For Gas activists. If successful this would destroy young lives, make people homeless and put them in debt for the rest of their lives. The first few days of an online petition to get EDF to drop the case collected 50,000 signatures.

Any act more likely to raise public indignation I cannot imagine. If they proceed with the action, EDF will find they have shot themselves - and the gas industry - in the foot. Apart from what many see as an unacceptable assault on the British tradition of peaceful protest, it has also been claimed that EDF used the police in an unacceptable way to provide them with information and even deliver civil action papers on protestors. Green MP Caroline Lucas was quick to react to these claims, asking the Secretary of State for the Home Department how policy applied to the provision of private data while criminal charges were pending (in the event all the protestors pleaded guilty), service of civil papers on the defendants, or whether this was in breach of procedures and policies.

EDF is no stranger to lawsuits. In November 2011 two EDF executives went to jail for spying on anti-nuclear activists Greenpeace, and the company had to pay £1.3 million in compensation. In February 2012 the High Court threw out a legal action by EDF against the group Stop Hinkley from entering its land or encouraging others to do so. No evidence had been presented to suggest Stop Hinkley intended to encourage illegal activity.

On the 18th February 2013, at the same time the news was breaking about EDF's attempt to claim 5 million pounds in damages from protestors, the Guardian newspaper announced that the UK government was involved in a "last-ditch" effort to resurrect the moribund nuclear power industry. As part of the package it is estimated as offering 50 *billion* pounds in subsidy to French firm EDF, in clear breach of a 2010 coalition agreement that no public subsidy would be given to encourage new nuclear power stations.

Looking at the wider British Isles situation, a host of groups have sprung up to oppose fracking and extreme/unconventional energy. These include Anti Fracking Network, Britain and Ireland Frack Free (BIFF), Rising Tide, No Fracking UK, Frack Off, Fracking Hell, North-West anti-fracking hub, RAFF, REAF, Refracktion, Frack-Free East Cheshire, Frack Free Sussex, Gas Drilling in Balcombe, No Fracking Cowden, SEER (Sussex Extreme Energy Resistance, East Kent Against Fracking, Deal With It (Kent), Stop Fracking Chatham Kent, No Fracking in Kent, No Fracking in East Kent, Frack Free Devon, Lingfield anti-fracking (Surrey), Frack Free Devon, Frack-free Somerset, Get the Frack out of the Mendips, Frome Anti-Fracking, Mendip Fracking Action, Saltford Environment Group, Frack Free Wales, SAFE (Swansea against fracked energy), The Vale Says No (Glamorgan), N.E.Wales Anti-Fracking Action Network, Frack Off Scotland, Frack Free Forth Valley, Central Scotland Sustainability and Climate Change Coalition, No Fracking Northern Ireland, Not For Shale (Belfast), No To Fracking (NI), Stop Fracking Fermanagh, FANN (Fermanagh Fracking Awareness Network), What the Frack (Irish cross-border), No Fracking Ireland, Fracking Free Ireland, No fracking Leitrim, No fracking Tyrone, and no doubt others. These groups have a huge potential to mobilise public opinion and share information too with a growing network across the US, Australia and other countries.

Other groups like Friends of the Earth, Greenpeace, the Transition Network, the Council for the Protection of Rural England, WWF and other animal and countryside protection groups all have a role in opposing fracking at a national level and also by local groups becoming involved in anti-fracking coalitions, as Frack Free Somerset have demonstrated.

We can also expect to see more involvement of student groups. Students at Lancaster University recently (February 2013) demonstrated against the Uni's plans to liaise with (i.e. accept money from) Cuadrilla in a joint business partnership venture. We've already seen that the Lytham St Annes police have an interest in videoing harmless peaceful meetings in order (no doubt) to provide activist information to security forces. It seems in the growing realisation that protests against fracking could eventually develop into a public order issue the police are mobilised. "Police and Community Support Officers were seen around campus throughout the day in what appeared to be a pre-emptive bid to maintain decorum whilst the talks were in progress", according to SCAN, the University's student newspaper. Lancaster University had played host a few weeks earlier to Professor Mike Stephenson. Presumably the students were not convinced by his pro-fracking argument.

Brighton Council led the local authorities who were ready to declare themselves a fracking free zone. Preston declared itself willing to pursue a frack-free policy.

But it is hard to avoid the conclusion that in the Fylde, with a Conservative MP, a Conservative-led County Council and a Conservative-led Borough Council the fracking protest movement can not expect much help there. Without a lot of support, effective mutual co-operation and coordination the prospects for the local campaigners seem gloomy. At the end of the day fracking may fail, due to national concern and frustration leading to widespread direct action and mass demonstrations. But in the meantime the Fylde will have been fracked and its future put at risk.

APPENDICES

Appendix A - University research - who pays?
Appendix B - See you in court?
Appendix C - The UK power circle

Appendix A - University research - who pays?

In the light of US fracking companies being unwilling to share information, rendering much scientific research impossible, and in the light of the limited information resulting from litigation, it is no wonder that much evidence of the harm fracking can cause is open to attack as "anecdotal". But evidence there is in plenty, and not all studies are dependent on the co-operation of the frackers.

As much research is centred on universities, and as universities in practice require funding from private as well as public sources for research projects, the question opens up just how far does project sponsorship skew outcome. In an ideal world academic research would be unbiased. But it is not an ideal world.

In October 2010 Jennifer Washburn produced a report for the Center for American Progress entitled "Big Oil Goes to College". This was an analysis of ten research collaboration contracts between leading energy companies and major U.S. universities.

The summary concluded *"In short, the 10 contracts examined in this report indicate that the balance between Big Oil's commercial interests and the university's commitment to independent academic research, high-quality science, and academic freedom seems to have tilted in favor of Big Oil."*

The report expresses some concern about outcomes of its own research. The fact is that in most of the contracts the university handed academic project selection to the corporations, gave up majority control of projects and in four cases gave full control to the participating corporations. None of the contracts required peer review. The universities kept the right to publish, but were bound to long publication delays (in order to give the corporations time to register patents), and the universities' ability to broadly licence the results of research were limited.

The report notes that in a time of economic difficulty and restraint, government is increasingly looking to lever private funding for research. The private sector, in return for its money, is looking for the expertise of universities, the kudos of university research rather than its own in-house research, and, not insignificantly, to establish for its own profit, new strong monopolies. It can also exploit its university connections to green its public image. BP and Exxon Mobil have made the most of this, and spent millions in advertising their partnerships.

The money spent is a drop in the ocean for these companies. BP's expenditure of $500 million in the Energy Biosciences Institute (an initiative of Berkeley UCB, the University of Illinois and the Lawrence Berkeley National Laboratory) is a mere 0.021 percent of BP's projected revenues and 0.26% of its projected profits over the years 2006-2015.

At the same time that the major oil companies put money into university research, they are spending millions in advertisements warning about the dire consequences of capping carbon pollution. Given that much of the new academic research is directed at new and low-carbon technologies, it might be asked how sincere is the industry's interest in greener technology.

Regarding the public contribution, according to Big Oil Goes to College, public energy R&D spending is now down to 1.6% of all federal R&D, from a high of 18% during the oil crisis of the late 70s and 80s. When there is an urgent imperative for climate change solutions, this figure is abysmally low.

Another point worth noting is that much of the publicly-funded academic research referred to involves biofuels, which remain controversial, and are criticised for effects on food production, food prices, poverty and livelihoods, and land use and soil erosion.

John DeCicco, of the University of Michigan, is quoted in the BOGC report as highlighting the essential problem of the public/private partnership in university research strategy - it inherently threatens the essence of public-good research. It blurs the lines between independent invention and analysis, and commercial R&D.

If we turn from industry influence on academic research into alternative energy sources, and look at research into the more practical side of conventional energy and strictly fracking-related issues, the concerns mount.

With the growth of the US and worldwide anti-fracking movement and the industry's attempts to dig in and retrench, new reports are appearing with increased frequency. The rush to deny claims of the antis is possibly leading to an increased incidence of flaws, adding confusion to the arguments for and against fracking, rather than resolving them. 2012 brought new scandals relating to the links between university research and the oil industry.

As a first example, in February 2012 a report authored by Professor Charles Groat at the University of Texas Energy Institute was published - "Fact-based Regulation for Environmental Protection in Shale Gas Development."

Key findings of this report were said to be (by Marcellus Drilling news et al):

"Researchers found no evidence of aquifer contamination from hydraulic fracturing chemicals in the subsurface by fracturing operations, and observed no leakage from hydraulic fracturing at depth.

"Many reports of groundwater contamination occur in conventional oil and gas operations (e.g., failure of well-bore casing and cementing) and are not unique to hydraulic fracturing.

"Methane found in water wells within some shale gas areas (e.g., Marcellus) can most likely be traced to natural sources, and likely was present before the onset of shale gas operations.

"Surface spills of fracturing fluids appear to pose greater risks to groundwater sources than from hydraulic fracturing itself.

"Blowouts — uncontrolled fluid releases during construction or operation — are a rare occurrence, but subsurface blowouts appear to be under-reported."

Hardly a whitewash for the process, but it was seized on for its claim that fracking did not contaminate groundwater.

The report, if you read the detail, is not as clear-cut as some of the critics - or supporters - said. One does wonder why a report searching for facts spends the first dozen pages looking at a survey of newspapers and media coverage of fracking and a public opinion survey.

But complaints about the report, including one from the Public Accountability Initiative, led to the University commissioning a trio of experts to look at it. Their remit was not to approve or contest the report detail, but to comment on its production and dissemination.

The PAI, in their own words, say, "We are a non-profit, public interest research organization investigating power and corruption at the heights of business and government." They accused principal investigator Professor Groat of being in the pocket of the oil industry. Specifically they said that he had received material compensation through his association with Plans Exploration and Production, a firm involved in hydraulic fracturing activities. Professor Groat confirmed the detail to the review committee.

The review team came to the conclusions that the study's design, management, review and release fell short of contemporary work standards. A primary shortcoming was Professor Groat's failure to disclose a conflict of interest. This was exacerbated by the University's policy on conflicts of interest, which was poorly constructed and even less well enforced. But they also criticised the report for its summary, press release and presentation not reflecting in a balanced fashion the caveats presented in the body of the report. The review committee found no evidence of intentional misrepresentation, but were critical of poor judgement "coupled with inattentiveness to the challenges of conducting research in an environment inevitably fraught with conflict of interest concerns." They commented that the university itself should pay attention to scepticism of its activities in energy research, "given that a non-trivial portion of its funds, trustees and members of the Energy Institute's Advisory Board are affiliated with the energy industry."

This last point is crucial. If the public perception is that fracking *is* causing problems, yet the industry denials are argued on anecdotal evidence, and then the industry pays academics who are seen as having their fingers in the till to produce reports justifying those denials, the industry can hardly complain about its reputation.

For Professor Groat the report signalled the end of his career at the University of Texas. He resigned later in 2012. Presumably he still retains his seat on the board of gas drillers Plans Exploration and Production. It is not clear whether he lost his annual fee ($58,000 in 2011, and totalling over $400,000 since 2006) from the gas drilling company. If so presumably he will be comforted by the value of his holding in the company, valued by Bloomberg at $1.7 million dollars in July 2012.

Another significant point raised by the review committee was about the presentation of findings. And this is far from being only of academic interest.

The report criticised the summary as misrepresenting the detail. This is an extremely important factor. Many readers of technical reports, including the press, will never get beyond the "executive summary".

In June 2012 in the UK The Royal Society and The Royal Academy of Engineering produced their report "Shale gas in the UK: a review of hydraulic fracturing". This was produced at the government's request, and came at an important time, when Cuadrilla's operations had been suspended and concern in the UK was mounting over the realisation that soon fracking might become a reality in the British countryside.

The media - especially the right wing - seized on the report's summary and proclaimed it as giving the green light to fracking. With adequate regulation in place fracking could and should go ahead. This completely overlooks the fact that a careful reading of the report makes it obvious that the verdict was not as clear cut as the media suggested, and further that the RS& RAE had inserted caveats in the detail texts which make their view plain that current regulation in the UK was inadequate and that regulatory authorities were not properly funded or well enough organised and coordinated.

These points were, of course, lost on the UK pro-frackers, who were able to use the media reports to fuel their pro-fracking arguments. Sadly, one wonders how many of the country's MPs actually sat down and read this report, and how many instead relied on either the media or their leadership's optimistic interpretation of it. Just like the Groat report's press release headline *"New Study Shows No Evidence of Groundwater*

Contamination from Hydraulic Fracturing", the Telegraph's " *Fracking should go ahead in Britain, report says"* was a distortion that many will still, unfortunately, believe.

Another example of a US university's vulnerability to manipulation by the oil industry is the University at Buffalo. In late 2012 president Satish K Tripathi announced he was closing down the Shale Resource and Society Institute. Again the decision followed an internal assessment following problems relating to non-disclosure of interest.

A report issued on May 15th 2012 said that state regulation in Pennsylvania had made shale drilling there far safer. But again concerns were raised by Public Accountability Initiative, and the issue was taken up within the university by English professor Jim Holstun.

The university was accused of putting its name on a citation of non-university research, and claiming falsely in a press release that the study was peer reviewed. The interests of authors T J Considine, an economist at the University of Wyoming, and R W Watson, an associate professor emeritus of engineering at Pennsylvania State University were not fully disclosed. The Institute's own co-director John P Martin was the third co-author. He works in planning and PR for the industry through JP Martin Energy Strategy. The Marcellus Shale Coalition, a trade advocacy group of oil and gas companies, financed studies by Dr. Considine and Dr. Watson on the economic impacts of natural gas development, according to the New York Times.

The Coalition also paid for three studies from Penn State University, to the tune of $148,000. However, a fourth study was aborted when several Penn State faculty members withdrew. The first three reports were co-written by Tom Considine (who since left Penn State for Wyoming) and failed to disclose their industry funding.

In the UK central government funding for energy research has also declined dramatically since the 1970s. At that time the majority went into nuclear fission - we may ask what happened to all that -

but now the annual figure has decreased from a high of some £1200 million per annum per year to under £100 million. A majority of this research funding still goes into fossil fuels, despite the imperative of tackling climate change.

An indication that the UK is in the same dire situation as the US when it comes to the potential risk of industry distortion of academic aims and results can be gauged from news in November 2012. The headline was this (Expertise Wales et al):

"Government funding boost for world-leading energy research at Swansea University"

Swansea University welcomed the announcement that it was to receive £12m of UK Government funding to develop the UK's first Energy Safety Research Institute. The total funding for the project would be £38m. Good news? Read on.

"The primary sponsor will be British Petroleum (BP)."

David Willetts, Minister for Universities and Science, said: *"It is fantastic that our top businesses and top charities are queuing up to collaborate with our world-class universities. They want to work together to deliver innovation, commercialisation and growth, which will help make sure the UK competes and thrives in the global race. This excellent project between Swansea University and BP will tackle the key issues we face."*

It is unavoidable to assume that the UK is going - or has already gone - down the same road as the US.

The CV of Professor Richard Davies, director of the Durham Energy Institute (which also has close links with BP) is not untypical. From 1986 to 2003 he worked for the oil industry, first as a trainee engineer and then as a geologist. In 2003 he joined Cardiff University as a senior lecturer, moving to Durham in 2006 and assuming a position as Professor of Energy and Director of Durham Energy Institute in 2010.

It would be unsurprising if Professor Davies' research results and media comments did not express his industry background, and therefore lead some critics of fracking to paint him as an industry spokesman. I would disagree.

In his work so far he has shown that not to be the case. He has expressed - at least in scientific circles - evidence of an open and enquiring mind that brings up some interesting questions that the industry would rather not have answered, for example the long-term fate of the fracking chemicals, and why the Eola field and Blackpool produced "exceptional" seismic results. He has also illustrated the need for a baseline in order to be able to distinguish between "natural" and "unnatural" contaminants in groundwater. And he has highlighted his concern about disposal of fracking fluid waste. An interesting question he has raised is that of subsidence, an issue which has so far been shouted down by the frackers, and remains below the radar of most anti-frackers.

But - at Imperial College, London, Professor Richard Selley displays a less open mind. He has been described (by the College's Department of Earth Science and Engineering) as one of the UK's best-known and most highly respected sedimentologists. As was hinted earlier, by reference to his evidence to the ECCC, he has shown himself to be an ardent supporter of shale gas exploration. Again unsurprising, as his experience includes years working for oil companies in, for example, Libya, Greenland and the North Sea, and presumably disappointment when his earlier research into shale gas potential was unrewarded. Now he sees attention returning to shale gas he is naturally willing to voice his backing to the media, and to anyone who will listen.

It is difficult to assess how Britain's universities will respond when they are called on to study fracking in the UK. To-date, necessarily, all they can do is deskwork looking at research from abroad.

An exception, of course, was the report the government required on the seismic dangers of fracking after the Blackpool experience. Or, rather, a review of Cuadrilla's own reports. The review team was: Dr Christopher A Green of Gfrac Technologies, Professor Peter Styles of Keele University, and Dr Brian J Baptie, of BGS.

Gfrac Technologies describes its activities thus:

"GFRAC Technologies provides a range of services to ensure development success in both Conventional and Unconventional Reservoirs (Shale, Tight Gas and CBM)."

Professor Styles has research experience in plate tectonics and seismic activity and is a past president of the BGS. His research at Keele is primarily in renewable energy and environmental problems.

Dr Brian J Baptie, of BGS we have met before. Needless to say BGS is partly dependent on oil industry funding, but I have seen no evidence of this interfering with the objectivity of its reports.

The report confirmed the findings that the Blackpool events were linked to Cuadrilla's fracking, and suggested a more robust regime to mitigate the chances of future seismic occurrences. The report attracted some criticism, and one of the authors, Peter Styles, has been accused of encouraging fracking by stating that it is capable of improving energy's security of supply, an opinion outside his scientist's remit. And he has said that with adequate regulation the risks of greenhouse gas production and seismic activity can be addressed. These are not statements that those opposing fracking want to hear, and are challengeable. But his views on other fracking issues are less credible. He follows the industry line dismissing the "gas in water" as evidenced in the film Gasland, and he made a curious statement as reported in the Agenda NI magazine, to the Northern Ireland Energy Forum. He said that hydraulic fracturing had been performed around 200 times since 1988, and the article said *"Sand is used as a 'propping agent' to keep the fractures open and he thinks that it is unlikely that other additives (to reduce the liquid's viscosity) will be permitted to be used in the UK and Ireland."*

This last statement is clearly untrue. Cuadrilla have already been "permitted" to use additional chemical additives in their fracking at Preese Hall. According to their website they have so far only used a friction reducer along with a "miniscule" amount of salt. They also state they wish to use polyacramide friction reducer, hydrochloric acid, biocide and sodium salt. These general terms hide the fact that each could be one of a wide number of different "products". So far Cuadrilla have specified the use in 2011 of CESI Chemical's FR-40 product, and Spectrachem's Chem Tracer. The concern, however, is not only what will happen in the future if Cuadrilla and others move on to exploitation rather than exploration, but what regulation there would be in place to ensure full disclosure of products and what checking the authorities would carry out to check adherence to the declaration. The evidence so far indicates the answer will be none to the latter question, and that the industry will be effectively self-regulating.

If not enough evidence is yet available on UK research into fracking for us to be comfortable or otherwise about the prospect of industry influence introducing bias into scientific reporting, the evidence is mounting that some of our academics are looking at the issues of fracking safety with an over-optimistic view of political reality. The government is showing little concern for the recommendations on regulation from the scientists it has employed to advise it. This topic is addressed later in looking at their response to expert advice.

It would be quite untrue to say all UK academics have their heads in the sand. In January 2012 Dr Robert Gross, director of Imperial College's centre for energy policy, said: *"The speed of shale gas exploration is running ahead of our knowledge of the risks, especially in America."* This is a warning that some of his colleagues should heed.

Appendix B - See you in court?

There have been many claims of damage to health and property in the US. Too many to list here. And many where litigation has been prevented by the industry coming to an out-of-court settlement with conditions of non-disclosure by the complainant.

Nevertheless some of the more rabid British pro-frackers, including UKIP's Chris French, make statements like:

"People will be aware that America is one of the world's most litigious societies, and if there had been serious environmental problems, the industry would surely have been closed down by class actions by now. In fact it is thriving."

This is both naif and factually erroneous. It ignores the fact that shale gas is comparatively new, and that a thriving and financially booming rich industry has never been deterred by payments arising from litigation. It also ignores the rising tide of litigation in the US.

So much money is involved in the energy industry that firms survive despite being forced to make occasional huge payouts. BP is still in operation, despite their financial responsibility for the Deepwater environmental spill disaster, which also resulted in loss of life. In November 2012 they pleaded guilty to criminal charges in a US court and agreed to pay $4.525 *billion* in fines and other payments for a criminal settlement. They are also paying compensation which might amount to a total of over $20 billion. One of BP's co-defendants was Halliburton, who have a track record of accusations of dubious practices including bribery, corruption, and a disastrous and notorious tenure of one-time CEO Dick Cheney. Halliburton Co is the world's largest provider of fracking services.

BP's Gulf of Mexico spill was not its first disaster. The 2006 Alaskan spill resulted in a court conviction for BP of (a mere) $20 million.

Head of BP at the time of the Alaskan spill was John Browne, Baron Browne of Madingley. He resigned as Chief Executive in

May 2007 following a scandal involving lying to a British court. But he had also suffered criticism for his role not only in the Alaska spill, but for being responsible for the original decisions and policies which led to the Gulf disaster, and subsequently caused the loss of billions of pounds from UK pension firms.

This did not prevent Lord Browne from being adopted by the Conservatives and installed into one of the most influential posts at the heart of government, where he remains to this day, with enormous power over government spending and decision-making. Lord Browne is also a major stakeholder in Riverstone Holdings LLC. Riverstone is of course a major owner of Cuadrilla.

It is simply not true that fracking is litigation free. Not only are people whose lives have been affected by fracking suing the companies and regulators. It works both ways. Now that states and government authorities are coming to take fracking seriously and put its operation under the microscope, the industry itself is taking legal action against government agencies to preserve its interests against what it sees as unlawful restriction or moratorium.

One of the reasons that litigation has not developed into what Chris French might see as damning evidence of fracking's problems can be seen by the Bloomberg BNA Daily Environmental Report, 26th April 2012, which confirms there is currently only limited federal legislation or regulation of fracking. It sees an increase in legislation as well as regulation inevitable, and suggests that this will impact on industry timescales and costs.

An article on Shale Development and Litigation Trends by Margaret Anne Hill, Mary Ann Mullaney and Heather L. Demirjian (The Legal Intelligencer July 31, 2012) suggests that despite what is now intense scrutiny and focus on environmental issues relating to US fracking, litigation has been slower to take off than expected. The article confirms that the majority of lawsuits alleging impacts on health and environment have been largely based on "common law" theories of liability. And different states have different requirements for satisfactorily making cases involving e.g. trespass, negligence, or public and private nuisance.

One difficulty that prevents successful pursuance of claims is that the onus is on the litigant to show factual data to prove harm done. This is almost impossible in many cases, and a particular problem in claims arising from leaking wells and release of toxic chemicals. How is it possible to make a case if you can not identify the offending chemical, and the fracking company will not release data of what they have used in their fracking chemical cocktails? Given that the companies reportedly (according to a Congressional Democrat investigation) use around 750 different chemicals in fracking this is a sizeable problem. Hopefully in the UK there will be requirement for full disclosure. But in the US there is still a way to go before the federal authorities or all state authorities require such disclosure. It is true that some states have passed disclosure laws, but, for example in Texas, complete disclosure is blocked by exemption claims. Company Superior Well Services, a subsidiary of Nabors, the largest US onshore drilling contractor by revenue, pumps EXP-F0173-11 into wells, but the lack of transparency and claims of trade-secret exemption mean regulations come up against a stumbling block. On a federal level, the EPA in 2010 asked nine companies for disclosures. Halliburton refused and answered a subpoena by saying they could not produce the information in the time given. The US experience, and a lesson for the UK, is that any system of voluntary disclosure is inadequate.

Until this is solved, successful or even attempted litigation will remain at today's levels. And we can be sure the fracking companies will be working to retain secrecy under the excuse of not releasing company-confidential information. The question has to be asked - if the fracking fluids are harmless, why maintain secrecy?

Nevertheless, there are documented examples of victories by claimants, even if under-the-counter. Michael Rubinkham reported via Associated Press on August 15th 2012 that residents of a north-eastern Pennsylvania town who said their well water was poisoned by fracking had their claim settled after a three year contentious federal lawsuit battle. Cabot Oil & Gas Corporation agreed a confidential settlement, which has been estimated at $4.1 million. Cabot had denied responsibility for polluting the residents' water supply by methane and toxic chemicals making some of the residents violently ill. State environmental regulators had however determined that Cabot contaminated the aquifer underneath Dimock with explosive levels of methane. The residents of Dimock still refuse to use their wells.

One 2012 settlement that was not hidden from view was the agreement by Chesapeake Energy to pay $1.6 million to three families in Wyalusing, Bradford County, Pennsylvania. The plaintiffs insisted they would not sign any confidentiality agreement.

The claim referred to contamination of the residents' water wells. The settlement included Chesapeake buying the families' homes, to help enable them resettle elsewhere. Chesapeake continued to assert the methane contamination was not caused by their drilling. Tod O'Malley, the attorney for the families, says his investigators concluded that a poor cement job was to blame. The residents began to notice problems after drilling started beneath their land.

The length of time it takes claims to go through the courts is another reason the list of resolved litigation is not as long as might be expected. This is true not only in the USA but in Canada.

In Alberta landowner Jessica Ernst has been suing EnCana Corporation and Alberta government regulators over water contamination. Since the case was filed in 2011 the tussle in court has involved legal technicalities, primarily whether claims should be struck and where the case should be heard. It is now proceeding in Calgary, for the convenience of the defendants' lawyers, rather than in Drumheller, which the claimant insists has the closest connection to the dispute - where the coalbed methane beds were drilled, and where her water was contaminated.

In the latest move (February 2013) the judge presiding over the case, Barbara L Vedhuis, has been shifted upwards to the Court of Appeal, effectively removing her from the Ernst case, preventing her from giving a judgement on whether the case should proceed and causing further delay until another judge is appointed to rehear the lawsuit. Ernst refused to be daunted, but said that the reappointment was another attempt to delay and exhaust her.

Although this case concerns CBM rather than shale gas, it illustrates the difficulties in pursuing legal claims which will apply equally to shale gas. It also an interesting case in that it demonstrates that it is not only the gas companies that are at risk from legal action, but the regulators. It also shows the disregard regulators show when their responsibilities are questioned.

ERCB, Energy Resources Conservation Board, has a legislative mandate "to ensure that the discovery, development, and delivery of Alberta's energy resources take place in a manner that is fair, responsible, and in the public interest."

Their 2011 Unconventional Gas Regulatory Framework—Jurisdictional Review states that their vision is *"to be the best nonconventional regulator in the world by 2013."*

They say:

"Much of the ERCB's current regulatory regime was designed for conventional oil and gas development and did not fully contemplate the unique nature of unconventional gas. As producers shift investment towards unconventional gas development, the ERCB needs to put effective regulation in place to address its development."

It would pay the British government to take particular account of this. The British law and oil and gas regulation was drawn up well before the advent of unconventional gas, even before North Sea gas, and is primarily a relic of the coal era.

"In support of its vision and mission, the ERCB has initiated a corporate-wide Unconventional Gas Regulatory Framework Project to develop and implement a new regulatory framework for the development of Alberta's CBM, shale gas, and tight gas by 2011."

Despite this vision, Ms Ernst is suing Alberta Environment for "negligent administration of a regulatory regime" by failing to take reasonable and adequate steps to protect householders from contamination of their water by the oil and gas industry.

The charge lists a number of detailed ways in which Alberta Environment and Alberta Energy and Utilities Board failed to take steps to prevent and identify water contamination, even when an issue was raised.

Again the British government and its regulatory bodies would benefit from considering how they can ensure not only that they have the strongest possible regulation in effect but can adequately police adherence to the regulation. UK regulation will be discussed in more detail in a later chapter, suffice it to say for now that despite the claims of government to the contrary, UK regulation is quite inadequate to deal with onshore shale gas exploration and production. And even the best regulation is inadequate. The oil and gas industry is not perfect. Mistakes will happen in even the best regulated industry.

It comes as no surprise to learn that Alberta and its regulator contest that there is no validity in any claim against them. ERCB argues that it is exempt from liability for its actions in the Ernst case and that it owes no "duty of care" to landowners impacted by oil and gas development.

Not even sound regulation, then, is adequate, it seems, to protect the public and the environment. Devising regulation needs a background of scientific knowledge and input, as well as common sense, but much of the knowledge is in the hands of the industry.

Can the US make progress in its own regulation? The problem has already been mentioned that federal regulation and law is weak, and left to the individual states there is a very patchy regulatory situation in the US.

In theory the federal US Environmental Protection Agency should be able, by carrying out and providing results of studies, e.g. on groundwater contamination, to make it clearer where responsibilities lie and make it easier for those harmed by fracking to pursue legal claims based on statutory rights. But the efforts of the EPA are being hampered by the spirit of non-cooperation from the fracking companies.

The EPA face not only opposition from the industry but from politicians. In November 2011 US Senator Jim Inhofe castigated the EPA for releasing a draft report that suggested that they had found compounds possibly related to fracking activities in groundwater. Inhofe is a senior Republican Oklahoma senator. In the 2008 election he received a total of $446,900 in donations from the oil and gas industry.

The EPA is obviously operating with one hand tied behind its back. If the frackers will not reveal what chemicals they use in their fracking fluids, it is unsurprising that they should only report what they find in groundwater as possibly the result of fracking. Bad science, according to Inhofe. Some of us might point the finger in the other direction and say bad law-making.

More recently the EPA attempted to put their research regarding fracking and groundwater contamination on a better footing, under Congress direction, with a progress report released in December 2012. The EPA's advisor Glenn Paulson described the project as *"one of the most aggressive public outreach programs in EPA history."* This includes talking to experts from the industry, the environmental community, and universities. However, the industry has been less than cooperative. The report will be unable to assess the statistical likelihood of contamination. It will have to rely on computer simulations of contamination rather than actual field tests. Why? It did not find one single company willing to test water content before and after fracking.

The rather depressing conclusion is that in the US there is neither adequate law nor adequate regulation to provide not only protection to the population but appropriate remedy when things go wrong.

Appendix C - The UK power circle

Mark Ruffalo, US screen star turned anti-fracking campaigner, said this about the underlying problem:

"We're clearly coming to the end of the fossil fuel era. We have the technology to shift to renewable energy, we have the will of the people. The only thing that's keeping us back is the fossil fuel industry's hold on our political system. That's what we need to change."

Ruffalo was talking about the US, but his words are an equally accurate description of the situation in the UK.

In the UK, the unprecedented threat to our countryside and environment has, fortunately, at last found recognition. Groups have sprung up all over the country, willing to tackle the shale gas industry head-on. They have already shown that they can be articulate and knowledgeable, and present a significant threat to the prospects of the industry.

But the movement against the introduction of fracking in Britain is up against some formidable opposition.

The big players in the oil and gas industry are not yet exercising their muscle directly, because as yet they have no big financial stake in fracking. This may soon change. Cuadrilla have been seeking funding partners, and it has been suggested that Shell, BP, Total S.A. and Statoil have been circling since the UK government flagged a restart for fracking testing after an 18 month moratorium. But this is still speculation, and the main drivers of pro-shale gas propaganda are Cuadrilla. They are a relatively small company, whose existing backers may bail out as soon as they get enough prospect of a major company buying in to maximise their investment, which has not been productive so far.

For all their claims, Cuadrilla can still not say whether if their testing proves encouraging they themselves would move forward to become key to the operating phase of shale gas exploitation. They have made no secret of this, admitting in their evidence to the

ECCC in 2011 that was too early to say. In one way, therefore, any assurance Cuadrilla can give about safe operation is meaningless. If they sell off their licence we will be in new hands.

But if Cuadrilla seem on the surface to have potentially less lobbying power than the big oil companies with their deep pockets, digging further reveals some disturbing facts.

At the end of the day it is the government decision-making which will determine the ease of fracking operations. And the UK government in the form of the present coalition between the Conservatives and the Liberal Democrats has shown it is not taking a neutral view on fracking, but is aggressively promoting the industry's interests.

This was made clear in a number of announcements in December 2012 and January 2013 - the go-ahead for fracking testing, tax breaks for the industry, and the threat of taking fracking planning decisions away from local authorities and hence local communities.

In view of this, it is worth asking how the UK government has come to its decisions, and what influences are at work. This illustrates not only how difficult it will be for local communities to resist the development of fracking, but how difficult it will be for anti-fracking viewpoints to sway those of politicians.

Against a background of economic problems, with no other ideas on policy to determine a positive economic strategy, the coalition has fallen for the idea that shale gas fracking will produce a new economic boom, benefiting the UK taxpayer in general, and boosting local economies where fracking takes place. It also promotes concerns about rising gas prices in the UK, even rather absurd claims that shale gas is necessary to "keep the lights on".

The Tory-led government is also cashing in on the fact that it is a coalition. The Liberal Democrats have, in theory, been the one among the three major UK parties which has demonstrated the greatest environmental awareness. But in propping up the Tories in order to gain some possibility of influencing green policy (in a charitable view) or for having their fifteen minutes of power (in the cynical view) they have allowed themselves to be rail-roaded into endorsing fracking. Many Liberal Democrat activists may be disappointed or even disgusted by that.

The reality has emerged that Conservative leader David Cameron's claims prior and post election promises to provide the "greenest government ever" were (predictably) nonsense.

Liberal Democrat Ed Davey was propelled into a position of environmental responsibility which is now seen to be a sham. Policy on fracking has not been dictated by the environmental issues but by hard-headed (and mistaken) economic imperatives.

David Cameron and George Osborne have bent those with more sensibilities to their will.

The Chancellor of the Exchequer has been a driving force behind not only encouraging, and promising to spend UK taxpayers' money on, shale gas - promising a "generous new tax regime" - but building new gas-powered power stations. Whether he will be as pro-fracking if the industry selects his constituency for their fracking attentions we will have to wait and see - the Tatton area sits over a potential shale gas basin.

Mr Osborne maybe improves his knowledge of the energy industry through conversations with his father-in-law, Lord Howell.

Lord Howell has a history of interest in the energy industry, including having been Secretary of State for Energy in the Thatcher era. Until a reshuffle in 2012 he was a Minster of State in the Foreign Office. Since then he has not been free of criticism. In January 2013 he was accused of a conflict of interest because of his paid connections with a Japanese train company JR Central. His son-in-law, days after the announcement of the go-ahead controversial HS2 rail project, went to Tokyo and said that Japanese bullet-train technology in which JR has an interest would play a part in HS2. Lord Howell is energy security advisor to Foreign Secretary and First Secretary of State and has access to the Foreign Office and confidential documents.

Although the conflict of interest row involved JR, Lord Howell also has a financial interest in the energy industry, being reported as working for the British Institute of Energy Economics, an oil and gas lobbying group, part funded by BG Group which has $200 million of investments in shale gas in the US. In June 2012 Lord Howell went to Poland - scheduled to become one of Europe's major shale gas countries - to promote British interest in Polish energy. Almost unbelievably, the Foreign and Commonwealth Office claimed in May that Britain had "developed a good process" on shale gas and wanted to share that with Poland.

In July 2012 Lord Howell was reported by the Daily Mail as having been forced to return £24,000 pounds he had taken as being "mistakenly" paid for a government job as FO advisor that he was supposed to be doing without pay. Lord Howell described the mistake as resulting from erroneous advice from officials. The Daily Mail said the blunder was "extraordinary".

In November 2012, the Independent newspaper was sent a video secretly recorded by Greenpeace, which included a conversation between an undercover Greenpeace activist with Lord Howell and Peter Lilley (a senior Tory MP known as a climate change sceptic).

Lord Howell claimed that his son-in-law was secretly manoeuvring to undermine the Prime Minister's climate change promises. He claimed Cameron did not understand the issues, but George Osborne was getting this message and putting pressure on.

Howell said that if the government was walking away from their climate change commitments he would "give them an extra push". The targets were "absurd".

It is made clear in the video that the Liberal Democrat Ed Davey was not "onside" but more "open to reason" than Chris Huhne, his predecessor, and if necessary the insider John Hayes was prepared to "duff him up".

Lilley said that Osborne privately regretted any green commitments that had been made and had used the recent cabinet reshuffle to facilitate ducking out of commitments that the government had "foolishly" made.

Peter Lilley had just been appointed to the Climate Change Select Committee, on the face of it an amazing decision. Lilley has been an avid opponent of wind farms, and an equally keen proponent of shale gas. His post as Vice Chairman and Senior Non-executive Director of energy company Tethys Petroleum netted him $400,000 of share options since 2007, according to a Guardian newspaper report. Tethys is a Cayman Islands based oil and gas company with drilling operations in Kazakhstan, Tajikistan and Uzbekistan. His remuneration by Tethys includes payments for advising on "business developments". The Guardian said that Lilley recently wrote a report – which failed to declare his oil industry interests – for Lord Lawson's Global Warming Policy Foundation, in which he criticised the "failings" of the influential Stern review of the economics of climate change published in 2006. In September, Lilley wrote to the BBC's director of editorial policy and standards to complain about the broadcaster's "systemic bias" in its climate change reporting.

Lord Lawson is a former chancellor whom George Osborne reportedly views as a hero. Lawson crossed swords with Osborne in July 2012 when he criticised the current Chancellor for too much time spent on Tory strategy and not enough on running the economy.

Lawson established and chairs the Global Warming Policy Foundation, a UK "think tank" whose job is to contest government policies to mitigate global warming. It has consistently refused to disclose its funding sources. There have been calls for the Charity Commission to review its charitable status in view of accusations of campaigning using factually inaccurate information.

Until the July spat it could have been assumed that Lawson's views carried some weight with George Osborne. Certainly climate sceptic Peter Lilley is on the same team.

The post of Environment Secretary is now in the pocket of the right-winger Owen Paterson. Like George Osborne, he has been an enthusiastic backer for the "dash for shale gas", and is known as another climate change sceptic, pro-fracking and anti-wind energy. Again it makes any sensible person wonder whether the environment is in safe hands with him holding the government's green brief. He has no track record of environmental issues or comments. Lord Lawson is believed to have endorsed his appointment to the job, with George Osborne planning to pack the government with supporters of his short-term energy dash.

To the further dismay of the environmentalists, John Hayes was given an appointment as minister in the Department of Energy and Climate Change, replacing Charles Hendry in the government reshuffle of November 2012. Hendry was fairly well respected as having some sensible views on energy. After his sacking he begged the Prime Minister to re-emphasise that low-carbon is an integral part of energy security, and urged the government coalition to get its act together and seal the growing rift between Osborne and Ed Davey. He emphasised the need to end uncertainty as vital to give confidence to investors in UK energy.

Hayes has no such qualms. He sees the issues as straightforward. He immediately launched a fierce attack on wind energy. His support for shale is not in doubt. Nor is his ability to make misleading, if not plain incorrect, statements about shale gas. For example using the US experience to imply shale gas will reduce consumer bills. And we have seen above other less-than-accurate statements he has made in the House.

The UK's sole Green MP Caroline Lucas has flayed David Cameron for his lack of control over his party. His campaign manager Charles Heaton-Harris was exposed as secretly backing a rival by-election campaign by James Delingpole, whose agenda is anti wind energy.

At the same time, and described as more troubling to Lucas, was the implication of John Hayes. It has been suggested that Hayes also conspired with Heaton-Harris and Delingpole.

Lucas accuses Hayes of showing nothing but contempt for DECC, run by Ed Davey, and contradicting DECC's position in press interviews. The conclusion to Lucas seems clear, Cameron has no intention of taking action against his party members and improving the chances of avoiding climate catastrophe.

If Lord Howell links George Osborne to pro-fracking influence, so do two other government peers with significant energy interests and significant influence.

Baroness Hogg is a director of BG Group, which has extensive US shale interests as well as Scottish contracts to buy fracked gas. She works for Osborne as a non-executive director at the Treasury.

That position was created by Lord Browne, who has a substantial stake in Cuadrilla.

Lord Browne occupies a hugely influential post at the centre of government. He has had an illustrious career, apart from his court appearances and the fact that he was held by some to have had some responsibility for BP's poor accident record.

He joined Riverstone as MD and partner in 2007 and is on the board of Cuadrilla Resources. He is said to have a very substantial personal stake in Cuadrilla's activities, apart from being chairman of the Cuadrilla board, and has been variously referred to as the "Fracking Czar" and "Sun King".

In June 2010 he was appointed by Francis Maude, Paymaster General and Minister for the Cabinet Office, as the government's Lead Non-Executive Director, charged with improving governance across Whitehall and bringing a more business-like approach to government.

A press release from the Cabinet Office described the position as a "key Whitehall role". His first responsibility was to work with Secretaries of State to appoint non-executive directors to the board of each government department. You can not get more central to government than that. For example Browne oversaw the appointment of four non-executive members to the Treasury - Baroness Sarah Hogg, Dame Deirdre Hutton, Sir Callum McCarthy and Michael O'Higgins. Three more of his appointees are at DECC, which grants oil and gas licences and oversees the industry. At DEFRA, the Department for Environment, Food and Rural Affairs, to which the Environment Agency is responsible, Browne has overseen the appointment of four non-executives. The list continues, appointees to the Cabinet Office, the Home Office, the Gas and Electricity Markets Authority (OFGEM), to a total of some

60 non-executives.

Does this matter, as fracking protestors suggest? Who knows, but it is undeniable that many who hold offices in government departments with involvement in the UK's energy policies, owe their jobs in part to one man who has a sizeable stake in fracking.

Browne's career in Whitehall has not been without problems. After two years, criticisms emerged. In August 2012 the Guardian reported that Browne appeared before the Commons Public Administration Select Committee and when asked if he expected departures he said not yet. Within four weeks two permanent parliamentary secretaries, Moira Wallace and Dame Helen Ghosh, had moved from the Home Office and DECC respectively. Dame Helen was rumoured to have left because of constant skirmishes in DECC , between DECC and the Treasury, in particular over cuts to wind farm subsidies. Another theory was disagreement with Ed Davey.

Ben Moxham has been Senior Policy Adviser on Energy and the Environment to the UK Prime Minister and Deputy Prime Minister since 2011.

Prior to joining Downing Street, he was a Vice President at specialist energy investor Riverstone Holdings, where he worked on renewable energy and gas investments in Europe, North America and South America. Mr Moxham spent the previous three years, from 2004-2007, at BP, first as head of external affairs for the company's petrochemicals and refining subsidiary, Innovene, and then as part of the team that launched BP Alternative Energy.

Further individuals with the ear of government include Guy Robinson who now works as advisor to, and was brought in by, Environment Secretary Owen Paterson. Robinson was previously head of political research at the Countryside Alliance, a group which proclaims itself as the voice of the countryside, but is effectively campaigning on hunting, shooting and fishing. Robinson worked also for the Australian Petroleum Production and Exploration Association, which included Australian gas company Dart Energy, CBM operators in Scotland, as a member. This appointment provides the opportunity for industry influence over the Environment Agency.

Lord Green was appointed Minister of State for Trade and Investment in January 2011. A Minister at the Foreign and Commonwealth Office, Lord Green works with Lord Howell (see above). He was appointed a non-executive director of BASF. Wintershall, the oil and gas arm of German chemicals group BASF, has said it is to explore for shale gas in Germany.

In December 2012 documents newly released under the Freedom of Information act revealed the degree of infiltration of DECC by the oil and gas industry.

Caroline Lucas, the Green MP who had made a number of the FOI requests, had previously expressed concern about this. A year earlier she had obtained documents which according to the Guardian showed that energy companies had "lent" more than fifty staff to government departments. The staff were provided at no cost to the government and worked within its departments for secondments of up to two years.

Since its creation in 2008, DECC had hosted 36 people from business and consultancies including EDF Energy, Centrica (parent company to British Gas), oil company ConocoPhillips, lobby group the UK Petroleum Industry Association and Energy Solutions, a US nuclear waste treatment company. Consultancies with major energy practices also supplied expertise, including KPMG and Ernst & Young.

The Department for Environment, Food and Rural Affairs had taken in 13 staff who work in the energy business, including three from EDF Energy, another from former British Energy, now owned by EDF, and employees from Npower and Shell.

Documents also revealed a substantial number of ministerial meetings with energy companies and lobby groups - 195 - against a total of 17 with green campaign groups between May 2010 and March 2011.

Further information now revealed about two dozen energy industry employees were working in DECC, and being paid by in most cases by the government.

The Guardian quoted Caroline Lucas as saying:

"Fossil fuel giants should have no place at the heart of government given that their current investment strategies run contrary to the need to build a low-carbon future that delivers both security and prosperity. It's even more outrageous that taxpayers are footing the bill for some of these secondments, including from British Gas-owner Centrica, at a time when British Gas customers are struggling in the face of a 6% rise in their energy bills, and the company is expected to make £1.4bn profits after tax this year.

"These corporations obviously don't lend out their employees without expecting something in return."

Acknowledgements

My particular thanks for permission to use material from web sites or quotes are due to - in no particular order -
Gayzer Tarjanyi, Frack Free Fylde, Andy Chyba, Mike Hill, John Hobson, Rebecca Roter, RAFF, Residents Action on Fylde Fracking (www.stopfyldefracking.org.uk), REAF Ribble Estuary Against Fracking (www.reaf.org.uk), Frack Off (www.frack-off.org.uk), Refracktion (www.refracktion.com), Fermanagh Fracking Awareness Network (FFAN), Ed Pybus Frack Off Scotland.

Other sources used in researching this book include the following -

Newspaper, media or web news sources –
The Guardian, Observer, Telegraph, Independent, Daily Mail, Financial Times, BBC, Reuters, CNN, CBC, News24, AFP, Bloomberg BNEF, Southport Visiter, Climatic Change journal, Journal of Geophysical Research, Huffington Post, Beacon Journal, Windsor Now, Marine and Petroleum Geology, Business Insider, Groundwater, Propublica, New York Times, Wales Online, This Is Bristol, Blackpool Gazette, Liverpool Echo, Lancashire Evening Post, Country Life, Sussex Argos, Archant KOS, Belfast Telegraph, Irish Independent, South Wales Evening Post, Scottish Herald and Sunday Herald, Newsnet Scotland, Airdrie and Coatbridge Advertiser, Associated Press.

Central and local government web sites, including sources of planning applications, commissioned reports etc -
DECC, Environmental Agency, HSE, gov.uk, DECC Seismic Report (Green, Styles, Baptie), Royal Society and Royal Academy of Engineering, Environment and Climate Change Committee, parliament.uk Hansard, Northern Ireland government, Lancashire County Council, Fylde Borough Council, European Union website - reports for environment and economy committees etc, West

Sussex County Council, Balcombe Parish Council, Bath and North East Somerset Council, Bridgend County Borough Council.

Other sources -
Cuadrilla Resources, BGS, Geological Society of London, Mark Menzies MP, Tyndall Centre Manchester, Friends of the Earth, Green Party Brighton, Bridgend Green Party, Imperial College London, National Grid, Cambridge Economics, Professor Robert Howarth, Cornell, Professor Anthony Ingraffea, No Hot Air (Nick Grealy), Oklahoma Geographical Society, Royal Lytham St Annes Golf Club, GWPREF, Duke University Durham NC, David Weaver Ultra Green, Alf Jan Wik WellCem, Dr Ronald Bishop State University NY, EPA, GAO, TEDX, NIOSH, OSHA, Dr Sheila Bushkin, University of Albany, Ecowatch, EHP, Professor Bernard Goldstein University of Pittsburgh, Colorado School of Public Health, Earthjustice, Refracktion, Pennsylvania Alliance for Clean Water and Air, Artists Against Fracking, CBI, Renewable Energy Association, OFGEM, gasdrillinginbalcombe, Bristol Rising Tide, counterbalance.org.uk, Blackpool Business Leaders Group, Center for American Progress, Professor Charles Groat University of Texas, GFRAC, Legal Intelligencer, Jessica Ernst, ERCB Alberta, Mark Ruffalo, Greenpeace, Frack Free Somerset.

Cover photo - Myke Treasure

MORE BOOKS BY ALAN TOOTILL

The Martin Cole Novels

Cole In The Country
Cole And The Cat Woman
Cole And The Corgi Killer
Cole And The Cactus Thief
Cole And The Clairvoyant

WRITING AS NICK POULTON

The Blackpool Novels

Marton Mere
Payback Call
Fracking The Fylde

For more information visit
www.alantootill.com

Printed in Great Britain
by Amazon.co.uk, Ltd.,
Marston Gate.